LIBRARY SERVICES FOR YOUTH WITH

AUTISM

SPECTRUM DISORDERS

LESLEY S. J. FARMER

ala editions

An imprint of the American Library Association
Chicago | 2013

Dr. Lesley Farmer, professor at California State University, Long Beach (CSULB), coordinates the Librarianship Program. She earned her MS in library science at the University of North Carolina, Chapel Hill, and received her doctorate in adult education from Temple University. Farmer has worked as a librarian in K–12 school settings, as well as in public, special, and academic libraries. She is incoming chair of the Education Section of the Special Libraries Association, and she is the International Association of School Librarianship's vice president of association relations. Farmer is a Fulbright Scholar and has received the Distinguished Scholarly Activity Award from CSULB, several professional association awards, and national and international grants. Farmer's research interests include information literacy, assessment, collaboration, and educational technology. A frequent presenter and writer for the profession, Farmer has published two dozen professional books and more than a hundred professional book chapters and articles.

Printed in the United States of America
17 16 15 14 13   5 4 3 2 1

Extensive effort has gone into ensuring the reliability of the information in this book; however, the publisher makes no warranty, express or implied, with respect to the material contained herein.

ISBNs: 978-0-8389-1181-5 (paper); 978-0-8389-9472-6 (PDF); 978-0-8389-9473-3 (ePub); 978-0-8389-9474-0 (Kindle). For more information on digital formats, visit the ALA Store at alastore.ala.org and select eEditions.

Library of Congress Cataloging-in-Publication Data

Farmer, Lesley S. J.
    Library services for youth with autism spectrum disorders / Dr. Lesley S.J. Farmer.
        pages   cm
    Includes bibliographical references and index.
    ISBN 978-0-8389-1181-5
    1. Libraries and children with disabilities. 2. Autism spectrum disorders in children. 3. Children with autism spectrum disorders—Books and reading.
    I. Title.
    Z711.92.H3F37 2013   ᘔ| 39
    027.6'63—dc23   2012027514

Book design in Mercury and Vista by Kimberly Thornton.
Cover image © Vanessa Nel/Shutterstock, Inc.

♾ This paper meets the requirements of ANSI/NISO Z39.48–1992 (Permanence of Paper).

LIBRARY SERVICES FOR YOUTH WITH

AUTISM

SPECTRUM DISORDERS

*To Maureen Sykes, who inspired me to write this book
and helped make it a reality*

contents

Developmental Characteristics of Youth with ASDs

THE TERM *AUTISM SPECTRUM DISORDERS* (ASDs) REFERS TO FIVE pervasive developmental disorders: autistic disorder, Asperger's syndrome, Rett syndrome, childhood disintegrative disorder (CDD), and pervasive development disorder not otherwise specified (PDD-NOS). Sometimes these disorders are categorized as "spectrum" disorders because the symptoms can range from mild to extreme; spectrum disorders are defined by linked subgroups of conditions rather than by a single characteristic. Because ASDs manifest in so many different ways, it is difficult to ascribe blanket characteristics to these children. A popular adage among people who work with youth with ASDs is "If you know one child with autism, you know one child with autism." Nevertheless, some aspects of these developmental disorders may be examined with confidence: sensory processing, communication, social interaction, and certain persistent patterns of behavior. Another important consideration is the developmental aspects of children of ASDs; they are growing individuals first of all. Furthermore, parental belief systems about lifestyles and treatment options can influence how parents treat their autistic children and interact with educational personnel.

Research into autism is ongoing, changing the face and scope of the disorder and the interventional treatments that ameliorate its symptoms. But it helps to have a solid understanding of the range of characteristics and behaviors of youth with ASDs in light of developmental issues.

ASDs AS THEY PLAY OUT IN DAILY LIFE

So how do characteristics of ASDs play out in the lives of youth with these disorders? Because these youth may react quite unusually to stimuli, they may exhibit particularly repetitive behaviors, which are their mechanisms for dealing with stimuli. Some children have difficulty controlling their behaviors within a high-stimulus situation; not surprisingly, most children with autism prefer predictable routines and environments. The online community Wrongplanet.net offers high-functioning youth with ASDs an opportunity to explore and share their feelings about the hardships of daily life:

> I am minding my own business, when my older brother nags me to go into his room and watch a video on his laptop, I hate being interrupted when [I] am doing something. But he then shows me these videos that he liked, or thought were funny, that I think are dumb, or boring. [And now] I am forced to use fake-emotions, and to hold my ever growing urge to tell him what I really think about the videos. . . . I am just going to stuff my head in my pillow and SCREAM!!!!! (iceveela, www.wrongplanet.net/postt172820.html, August 27, 2011)

Furthermore, what may be routine for some, such as playing ball, sometimes requires explicit attention and step-by-step concentration for children with ASDs. They may have difficulty imagining the perspective of another person. It should be noted that empathy is very present in autistics; it just presents itself differently. The following blog post by a young woman with ASD also underlines the potential role of libraries to work with these youth:

Now that I have the ability to recognize my difficulties and the tools to fix them, I am far more socially competent than I ever was before learning about autism. I used to be the stereotypical awkward misfit, never wearing the right clothes or acting the right way. I had no idea how to comfort a crying friend, or how to maintain a romantic relationship. I had no idea that there were people (and books) that could teach me, or that I was capable of learning! (Lindsmith, www .wrongplanet.net/article407.html, August 2, 2011)

Children with ASDs may seem to prefer to be alone, as they tend not to express easy-to-interpret feelings of affection; for instance, they may play side by side rather than interactively, which is their method of socialization. A commenter at wrongplanet.net noted:

My passion had always been art, and drawing taught me to read faces. I analyzed the muscle structure of the human face, and which places were contracted or relaxed in different moods. I was also pretty into anime and manga, which place a heavy emphasis on facial expressions. I feel sort of lame admitting it, but a lot of what I learned about non-verbal language came from my consumption of Japanese media as a teenager. The down side was the anime faces I started to imitate, thinking they were natural (Lindsmith, www .wrongplanet.net/article409.html, August 17, 2011)

Children with ASDs are usually developmentally impaired with respect to speech development, although some children may communicate well in other ways, such as by creating images or typing. Some youth may feel that their minds are running a mile a minute, too fast to articulate their ideas clearly; their thoughts outrun their words. To these youth, there seems to be a disconnect between their senses and their circumstances:

"I am me" is disconnected. . . . Even saying it now creates a feeling of disconnection. I hide behind something fake, this much I know is true. If I search inside for the me I know must exist somewhere[,] I can't reach it. I don't know what I'm looking for, so often I just feel numb. (Kiana, www.wrongplanet.net/modules.php?name =blogview&user=Kiana, August 25, 2011)

In a way, a case might be made that such youth have a hard-enough time trying to figure out how they themselves work, almost as if their bodies were misaligned with their minds and hearts. They have difficulty reaching the point of being comfortable enough with themselves to have the energy and wherewithal to predict how another person feels inside. In short, youth with autism are very much part of the world, and they are children first, before they are children with autism. To create a safe haven, librarians can serve as a resource center for these teens. Librarians can also gather information about adolescence and ASDs and post them on their web portal for teens to access independently. For instance, librarians can provide links to the following blogs and websites, which reflect the voices of youth with autism:

> *Autistic Female's Blog*: a girl's life on the autism spectrum (http://autisticfemale.com)
> *Babble*: lists thirty topical ASD blogs (www.babble.com/baby/baby-development/top-30-autism-spectrum-blogs/)
> *Carly's Voice: Breaking through Autism*: written by a teenage girl with autism (www.carlysvoice.com)

DEVELOPMENTAL APPROACH

As already noted, ASDs are developmental disorders, so it is useful to take a developmental approach when exploring how to work with these youth. In general, youth with ASDs lag in the areas of social, communication, and emotional development. It should be noted that other developmental issues may be involved with these disorders, such as cognitive development, but such issues are not necessarily specifically related to ASDs.

Social Development

The following areas of development occur in sequential progression over time. The areas here indicate age benchmarks for neurotypical children, although children with ASDs tend to lag developmentally in these areas (Hall 2009):

DEVELOPMENT OF SOCIAL SKILLS

1. **Orientation, onlooking:** child shows awareness of others by looking at them or their playthings; may imitate peers while looking from a distance; can sustain attention focus (typical at age one).
2. **Isolation:** occupies self by self-stimulation or watches something momentarily (typical at age two).
3. **Parallel and proximate play:** child plays in parallel rather than with peer; may show objects to or do alternate actions with peer (e.g., pushes a car beside a child who is building a road; typical at age three).
4. **Common focus:** child plays by interacting with peers; child demonstrates joint attention through joint action, mutual imitation, and reciprocal social exchange (typical at age four).
5. **Common goal:** child engages in structured play with peers to attain a common goal or make something, such as a building; negotiates behavior exchanges and complementary actions; demonstrates cooperation and group belonging (typical at age five).

DEVELOPMENT OF SYMBOLIC PLAY

1. **Nonengagement:** child does not touch objects; self-stimulates (typical at six months).
2. **Sensory manipulation:** child manipulates objects without conventional purposes; seeks sensory input and control over objects; performs feats and action sequences with single or combined objectives (typical at eighteen months).
3. **Functional play:** child uses objectives conventionally and follows familiar routines with realistic props (typical at age three).
4. **Symbolic or pretend play:** child plays in a representational style in terms of role or action (e.g., holding a pretend plate, drinking from an empty glass, acting out bedtime with dolls) (typical at age six).

Techniques to help children progress to the next developmental social stage of symbolic play include the following:

- Arrange the environment to facilitate exploration and social interaction.

- Provide an obvious theme or purpose for action.
- Weave desired learning opportunities into daily life.
- Choose a highly motivating activity, such as using a favorite toy to learn a concept.
- Plan for repetitive action and ways to provide variations in that action (e.g., rolling a ball at different distances, rolling different objects).
- Structure action to support taking turns in predictable sequences, such as providing only one object that needs to be shared (e.g., a ball).

Communication Development

Language is a keystone for structuring the human brain, which creates mental schemes to make meaning of the surrounding world, to communicate and learn with others, and to survive in society. Language development depends on physiology as well as environmental conditions and social interaction.

Youth with ASDs exhibit several communication issues and delays: echolalia (i.e., repetitive wording), unexpected tone of voice, unusual vocalizations, lack of understanding of word boundaries and a tendency to comprehend phrases as single chunks of speech, and difficulty generalizing the meanings of words. Several communication behaviors are typical for youth with ASDs:

- social communication according to their own standards, such as not using social greetings
- little appreciation of the need to share information but expression of his or her own needs
- verbosity (and ability to manipulate conversations) on a topic of interest
- limited shared enjoyment of social situations, perhaps with just a few adults
- preference for talking *to* another person rather than *with* that person
- poor understanding of others' gestures
- little use of gesture, intonation, and nonverbal expression
- idiosyncratic use of words and phrases

- prescribed content of speech, such as answering a welcome the same way every time
- no spontaneous response
- apparent lack of hearing
- literal understanding of words and phrases
- poor grasp of subtle jabs, irony, or sarcasm
- poor grasp of abstract concepts and feelings
- expression developed before understanding

Emotional Development

To some, youth with ASDs may seem emotionally "flat." In general, they do not like being touched, which is one way people often express emotion. Furthermore, they have difficulty reading body language and using body language to express emotion. However, youth with ASDs do have strong feelings, but they cannot always articulate or control them according to social norms because of sensory and motor impairments.

EARLY SIGNS OF ASDs

Although ASDs might be diagnosed in adulthood, their manifestations are almost always present by age three. It is possible to make a false diagnosis of autism early on; however, it is usually better for parents to seek developmental interventions—such as structured activities to build social relationships—than to ignore telltale signs. Even babies' behavior may indicate possible signs of ASDs, such as unusual quietness, extreme irritability and resistance to soothing, or nonreaction to significant others (Cohen 2007).

AS YOUTH WITH ASDs GROW UP

A young person with an ASD is, first of all, a young person. Even though he or she has to deal with some delays in communication or social behavior, his or her other physical development may be typical in many ways. In addition, the child is likely at some time to play with some age-appropriate toys and to be in the same environment as his or her peers, such as at home or school. As the child grows up, the way that an ASD affects his or her life also reflects the world in which he or she has to navigate. That world can include the library, as it provides a neutral and accepting learning environment with a variety of resources that can address young people's specific interests.

Preschool Years

Preschoolers with ASDs display a variety of behaviors, which may also depend on any other disabilities they may have, such as learning disabilities or seizure disorders. Some may seem like little adults, whereas others may appear passive or aggressive. Most preschoolers with ASDs do connect with a few people, most likely their parents or another adult, largely because the adult can figure out the child's intent and is able to fulfill the child's request. The child might not hug the adult or look him or her in the eye, but a relationship exists. Parents can introduce librarians to their child to start that relationship.

Most preschoolers with ASDs limit communication to personal needs, and they may have physical difficulties producing speech. Adults need to use language that is within the child's range of understanding. In some cases, preschoolers with ASDs may be hyperlexic—that is, they have the ability to read at an early age, but they are more able to recognize a word-pattern image rather than understand the meaning behind the words. If a child articulates a word without meaning, the adult can help the child make the appropriate connection between the sound and the meaning. Note that a child may obey a command or follow a direction not because of the vocabulary but because of the routine associated with a location. In this way, parents can help librarians by explaining how their child prefers to communicate, and the librarian can share some basic library terms, hopefully matching the child's communication mode, such as by using a visual signal.

Many preschoolers use echolalia: repeated words or phrases, sometimes echoing what another person says. They may like the sound of the words, repeat phrases as a way to rehearse meaning, or have a pleasant association with the words and their connotations (e.g., SpongeBob SquarePants, "Off to Grandma's!"). Preschoolers with ASDs tend to use echolalia more pervasively than other preschoolers and continue to use echolalia for years, and they may make unusual associations between a phrase and meaning (usually with delayed echolalia), such as "Help me, Obi-Wan Kenobi!" and wanting popcorn, because the child had popcorn once when watching *Star Wars* some time prior. Knowing the connection between the phrase and the meaning helps adults, including librarians, and peers better interact with the child, and they can redirect the phrase by saying, in this instance, "Do you want popcorn?"

Preschoolers with ASDs are likely to display distinct play behaviors. They may play by themselves but not necessarily alone. A child may be amusing himself on the edge of a big sandbox or in a section of the library, with other children playing together elsewhere in the same space; the child with ASD probably believes that he is part of the scene and is comfortable with the play arrangement. Again, such behavior is typical for all three-year-olds, but preschoolers with ASD may continue such play behavior for years. Because of this, ASDs sometimes are not diagnosed until age five or later.

As mentioned before, a preschooler with ASD might have already developed specialized interests; use play objects in unusual ways; or focus on details rather than the whole, such as spinning a toy car's wheels instead of moving the car itself. Such specialization is fine, as long as it is safe and socially appropriate, and it can be used to motivate children to learn. However, adults should encourage children to expand their interests and stretch their comfort zone before too much rigidity sets in. Librarians can start by providing resources that meet the child's interest and then link those resources with others.

As with other children, adults should help preschoolers with ASDs get ready for formal education by helping them learn self-care routines (such as hygiene and dressing) and basic social—and library—skills (such as greeting others, saying one's name, and self-regulating anger).

Elementary School Years

Children with ASDs start to diverge in their functionality and interests in elementary grades; some gain language skills that signal Asperger's syndrome, whereas others display disabilities, such as physical ailments.

Both cognitive and emotional changes occur in elementary years. Mental functioning shifts between the ages of five and seven as children start to think more logically and recognize codes of social behavior. At the same time, more aggression and self-injury may occur, as these children often have a harder time copying complex sets of behaviors or being required to transition from one activity to another.

In terms of language, some children with ASDs may understand language (i.e., be language receptive) but might not speak much, or they may be able to read aloud a text without comprehending it. Because some children with ASDs may tend to speak little at all or in long monologues without anticipating how other people will react, they may need explicit training in how to converse, including identifying a topic, paying attention to what another person says and responding appropriately, taking turns speaking and listening, using appropriate body language, and ending a conversation. Children with ASDs may need to consciously learn and memorize what comes naturally for other children. Even children with Asperger's syndrome, who usually know when it is inappropriate to talk, may have difficulty changing their language patterns to fit the type of listener, or they might interpret others' behaviors in terms of their own natural action rather than trying to understand a different point of view.

These social and communication behaviors can make it harder for children with ASDs to make friends. However, these children might not feel a great need to have close friends. Nevertheless, adults should encourage the child's peers to interact with one another and should designate a part-time buddy or two for these children to ensure that they have social friend experiences. At the same time, adults need to respect a child's need for greater personal space and not push closeness. The library provides a welcoming yet neutral social space in which children with ASDs can find a comfortable corner.

In elementary grades, children with ASDs are likely to display special abilities in memorization, spatial concepts, math, technical activities, music, or art. They may also be experts in specific topics, such as cars, seashells, sports statistics, or cartoon characters. About 10 percent of children with ASDs may be considered savants (i.e., have extraordinary abilities in specialized areas, such as music). Hopefully, libraries have collections that can support these children's specializations.

Preteen Years

Middle school can be a difficult time period for children with ASDs. They usually have enough self-awareness to know that they are different, but they tend to be vulnerable and guileless. Social norms can seem very strange to middle schoolers with ASDs. What is the right clothing to wear? What is the right thing to talk about? Not only are acceptable norms rigid, they can change with seemingly arbitrariness. Although most middle schoolers with ASDs could not care less about these details, their peers may be very intolerant of such "nonnormal" behavior and snicker or taunt them. At this period in life, boys with ASDs are most likely to be bullied because they have difficulty managing emotional responses and understanding their peers. From an adult's point of view, the rigidity of some youth with ASDs seems perfectly in step with that of other preteens.

Social interaction is particularly hard for early adolescents, and even more so for those with ASDs. Children with ASDs may have a couple of friends, but those friends may quickly reject them. Middle school cliques form and break up regularly, much to the dismay and puzzlement of children with ASDs. Large-group free-form socialization, such as lunchtime, can be overwhelming for middle schoolers with ASDs; librarians and other educators can help these children by talking with them about ideas for ways to deal with lunchtime, such as finding a designated table or starting a social lunch club in the library to discuss their favorite pastime or interest. As with elementary grades, having a designated peer buddy can provide predictable and safe companionship. Older siblings can also help children with ASDs socialize.

In addition to social interaction, middle schoolers with ASDs have to deal with their own changing physiology, which they cannot control. Girls often have a difficult time dealing with menstruation, boys have to deal with changing voice range, and both sexes have to cope with "grown-up" genitalia. Some boys are even sent to the principal's office because they get erections that they don't understand except as pain and are ridiculed by their peers. In addition, emotional mood swings can unsettle these youth—along with their families and others. As much as possible, caring adults should prepare children for such changes and give them "scripts" on how to deal with them. Most youth with moderate to severe autism have paraeducators or shadow aides who follow them throughout the day and assist with these life transitions.

Librarians should work with these assistants to smooth out experiences for these preteens.

Teenage Years

Teenage experiences vary greatly for youth with ASDs. Not only do their own behaviors become more idiosyncratic, but their situations and interactions can reflect more acceptance or more conflict both on their part and from others.

Many teens with ASDs continue to have limited language skills or other communication impairments, and they are likely to have some ritualistic behaviors. They often think literally, so they are less likely to understand jokes, sarcasm, or irony (which is a big factor in teen conversation). Not surprisingly, their social networks are usually small, and changes in that arena can be crippling. Depending on the interventions taken earlier on, some teens, especially those with Asperger's syndrome, might not qualify for special education services anymore at this age because their intelligence and behavior are consistent. Some teens with ASDs may also become less rigid and more tolerant, thus fitting in more easily. Furthermore, as they grow older, they may find small groups of people with similar interests so they can combine personal interests and social affiliation (e.g., Trekkies, rock hounds, coin collectors).

However, many teens with ASDs experience worse problems and emotional turmoil during the teenage years. As social and academic challenges become more sophisticated and complex, their frustration levels may rise. The academic chasm may become so great that these teens are placed solely in special day classes and socialize only with other youth with special needs. Consequently, these teens miss out on social cues and behavior, which makes it more difficult for them to integrate into adult society. Self-soothing behaviors, such as rocking, may increase as an immediate response to troubling situations. Emotional and physical imbalances are common at this age. For example, teens may be "turned on" sexually but unlikely to touch others; teens with Asperger's syndrome are often asexual. Teens may experience depression caused by surrounding situations and exacerbated by hormonal extremes. Aggressive behavior may increase, becoming more disruptive and dangerous. Some teens with ASDs start having seizures, which may be linked to behavioral deterioration such as increasing compulsion and acting out (Cohen 2007).

More seriously, antisocial behavior may catch the attention of police and result in undue arrests; for example, these teens may exhibit extremely inappropriate behavior; cause offense without being aware of other people's reactions; appear aloof, egocentric, or insensitive; not know how to react to a situation or to others' feelings, be hard to understand, and use nonverbal communication; not like being touched; or have extreme intolerance of sensory input, such as bright lights (Plimley, Bowen, and Morgan 2007). Caring adults need to explicitly teach youth with ASDs how to react to authority in nonthreatening ways, particularly as many people in authority remain unknowledgeable themselves about the behaviors of youth with ASDs. For instance, librarians can teach library manners and rules, and can refer to them on posters or other signs; teens with ASDs may feel comfortable about such behavioral expectations, which apply to all library users.

Teens with ASDs need to be independent, and most want such experiences of independence, just like other teenagers do. For instance, they usually prefer to shop with peers than with their parents. They should participate in household chores as a way to transition to independent living, starting with jobs that build on their natural affinities, such as sorting laundry or cleaning their rooms. As much as possible, teens need to learn adaptive behaviors and to replace maladaptive behaviors before they become too stuck in their daily routines at home. They can also practice independence in libraries, which provide developmentally appropriate supervision and guidance.

Transition to adulthood is another important issue for teens with ASDs and their service providers. In general, these teens have fewer career and life choices than other teens. Postsecondary education has less structure and more adult responsibilities, which can be hard to handle for them. Therefore, these teens need to learn life and career skills while still in high school. Teens transitioning to adulthood also need to learn workplace and societal norms, such as library functions, which differ from their schooling experience. They might need supported or residential placement, in which case they might have to share living space with strangers. If they live independently, they might choose a more isolated lifestyle. Furthermore, without school, social exclusion may occur, which can lead to social regression and social anxiety. Again, public libraries provide a lifelong public venue in which these youth can feel safe and competent.

THE LIBRARIANS' ROLE

By now it should be obvious that the world of a child with an ASD can be a scary, mysterious place, but warmth and educated support can make a world of difference. Librarians should try to get to know youth with ASDs on a personal level so they can provide more appropriate services.

As noted already, librarians and other service providers should emphasize daily living skills, emotional-social skills, and communication strategies. Library materials on these topics are very helpful, especially if they are literal and easy to read, and include clear realistic images. Librarians can also provide teens with positive work experiences helping in the library with such duties as shelving, technical installations, and other detailed work that matches teens' interests.

Librarians should be sensitive to the developmental stages of these children, both in light of ASD-specific characteristics and in terms of peer interaction and typical childhood behaviors. As information professionals, librarians should learn about ASDs and should help parents and guardians, other service providers, and the youth themselves find useful resources.

REFERENCES

Cohen, Shirley. *Targeting Autism*. 3rd ed. Berkeley: University of California Press, 2007.

Hall, L. *Autism Spectrum Disorders*. Upper Saddle River, NJ: Merrill, 2009.

Plimley, L., M. Bowen, and H. Morgan. *Autistic Spectrum Disorders in the Early Years*. London: Paul Chapman, 2007.

CHAPTER 1

Youth with ASDs in Libraries and Other Educational Settings

WHAT IF YOU WERE PUT INTO A MOVIE THEATER AND the lights were as bright as a football field during the movie? Or what if everyone around you had smoking, burned popcorn that assailed your olfactory senses? Or perhaps the people next to you are screaming? And what if there were gnats flying about, picking at your skin? This is an example of the constant world of the autistic child while seated in the classroom: it's overwhelming and all too much. They must wonder why we don't all sense things the same way they do, just as we wonder why they sense them too much.

Children with ASDs encounter challenges in libraries and other educational systems because they have impaired social and communication development. Social situations are very difficult for them because their social skills evolve differently. Moreover, ASDs affect children's thoughts, perceptions, and attention span. Their body language often differs from that of children without ASDs, so the two parties

1

may have problems "reading" each other. In addition, people with ASDs tend to think literally, so metaphors and idioms can present problems in communicating with them. Current educational thought promotes an inclusion or mainstreaming model of education; nevertheless, these children require special attention, because ignorance of ways to interact with them can result in frustration for all parties. Moreover, children with ASDs need more than an academic curriculum per se; they need extended instruction in socialization skills beyond the regular classroom rules. Thus, this chapter deals with the challenges that youth with ASDs face in library and educational settings.

A WORD ABOUT PUBLIC PLACES

Federal laws mandate that public spaces be accessible to people with disabilities. Ramps, universal handles, gate-free entrances, wide aisles, and signs are all examples of ways that buildings can accommodate special needs. However, such measures do not guarantee that people can use the facility purposefully. Each space has defining areas and an organizational scheme. For instance, a house usually has a living room, kitchen, bathroom, and bedroom. A grocery store has aisles of shelves filled with items, and the checkout area is usually located near the entrance or exit for supervision reasons. Within these general frameworks, furniture and smaller items are arranged according to the owner's scheme. Even in these simple examples, it can be hard for people to find what they want in those spaces.

Most public spaces are much more complex, and each public space has its own information scheme. Different types of public entities, such as a recreation center or a gas station, use spaces according to their unique function. Therefore, once a person is able to navigate one gas station, for example, he or she can usually figure out how to navigate a different brand's gas station, even though the details may differ between particular stations. In any case, users of a public space have to determine the facility's basic and possible ancillary functions. They have to identify the facility's rooms or separate areas, its physical features, and the furniture and other items therein. They also have to identify the spaces or passageways between the objects and figure out how to navigate through them to get from one area to another. Maps and information desks help, but these go only so far and might not scale down to the detail needed. Anyone who has tried to find a specific counter or form in a large complex such as a hospital can understand the difficulties involved in this.

In addition, public spaces are used by the staff and clientele of those spaces. The staff are more or less permanent, and the public is generally transitory, although some individuals may use a public space regularly. In general, the staff perform certain expected functions and are assumed to know what resources and services are available in the public space. The public generally comes to the public space to use those resources and services, although they are usually not experts on those things. The public thus has to figure out how to interact with the people, both staff and other users, in that public space. Each type of public space has its behavioral norms and expectations, just as it has generic space allocation. For instance, people are expected to behave differently in a baseball stadium than in an art museum in terms of voice, body movement, dress (to some degree), food habits, and human interaction. The objective or function of the public space determines those social norms. Just as one has to learn how to navigate and interact with a physical public space according to its function, one has to figure out the social norms of human interaction in those public spaces. Children tend to learn these norms under the guidance of adults, but they also learn from peers or discover norms through observation and subsequent trial and error.

So even though public spaces are supposed to be accessible to all, they might not be very accessible to youth with ASDs. For youth with ASDs, each space is a unique set of properties; it is difficult for someone with an ASD to make accurate generalizations from one space to another. One grocery store may seem completely different from another; one restroom may seem to function differently from another because of the arrangement and appearance of the objects in the space. A person with an ASD might focus on a specific detail, such as the low mirror under a seat in a shoe store, but not figure out that shoes are arranged by size within the store. Alternatively, a person with an ASD may find unlikely associations among seemingly dissimilar public spaces, such as mirrors in a shoe store, mirrors in a gas station restroom, and a doctor's head mirror.

Furthermore, some youth with ASDs have short-term memory problems, so they forget from one time to another how to use and behave in a specific public space. Signs and maps can be useful markers for youth with ASDs, probably more useful than an information desk at which one has to ask another person articulate questions. Nevertheless, youth with ASDs have to be explicitly taught how to analyze a public space and how to behave within it. Because so many public spaces exist in a community, such instruction can seem daunting not only to youth with ASDs but also to service providers and families.

LIBRARIES FROM THE VIEW OF YOUTH WITH ASDs

Libraries are usually public places that serve a variety of clientele. Any public place can be disorienting to children with ASDs, and they have to learn how to navigate that space, usually with the help of a family member or service provider. Even though libraries are considered orderly, to a child with an ASD, the library does not have the same order that he or she is used to at home. Furthermore, the library's functional scheme often does not reflect the internal scheme of youth with ASDs, even though they may be highly organized. Somehow, the two mental schemes have to be negotiated.

Whether a child with an ASD feels comfortable in a library setting might not depend too much on his or her prior experiences, be it at home or in another public place, because it is harder for children with ASDs to make transitions from one location to another. Thus, the child whose home lacks books or computers might not be disadvantaged in comparison to children with print- or technology-rich homes. However, it is possible that such children might focus on a favorite book displayed in the library that is found at home as well; certainly, librarians can let the child know that the book at the library is a different copy and that he or she can borrow books to read at home or at the library.

In any case, youth with ASDs benefit from individual orientations to the library, and they may need several orientations if they forget how to navigate the library. Usually a parent or other service provider accompanies the child to the library, staying with him or her throughout the orientation to help reinforce information about the library.

The library is, first, a place. What is in the library? What can be used in the library? Where can one sit in the library? The librarian may want to designate a seat for the child to provide a sense of predictability; however, the child might not want to share that seat when peers come into the library, so an alternative solution is to make a nameplate for the child and say that the seat is hers when the nameplate is placed on it. If the child likes and understands maps, using a map as part of the orientation is a good practice, and it helps the child act independently if the map is placed in a binder that the child keeps and uses regularly.

The librarian needs to explain the purpose of the library: using and borrowing (and returning) library materials. It is important to go through the circulation procedure step by step. Ideally, having a sequential chart or flip cards or incorporating photos or simple drawings helps *all* children know what to do. Other procedures—such as signing in or waiting until the bell rings to leave—also have to be taught step by step. These procedures can be made into posters and hung near the circulation desk. Likewise, the librarian needs to show children how to locate an item in the library, both by browsing and by using the library catalog. For youth who like numbers, the Dewey Decimal Classification (DDC) system might be an interesting piece of knowledge and a sign of orderliness in the library; librarians can also explain that many libraries use the same DDC system, so locating an item in another library can be simpler once the DDC is understood (although some youth with ASDs might not be able to make that mental transfer of knowledge to a different site). In any case, call numbers and other library organizational systems are the products of librarians' minds, so youth with ASDs have to conceptualize a different organizational scheme than ones that they are familiar with. Signs can help provide cues for popular parts of the collection. Librarians should note, though, that even if they point out where a child's favorite book or section is, such as graphic novels, the child may forget the location between library visits.

The librarian also needs to explain concretely how to act in the library: how loud to speak, how to ask for help, how to talk with others in the library, how fast to walk, how to handle resources, how to log in and log out, what to do with resources when done with them, and so forth. Children with ASDs may have a hard time understanding that they may have to sit at a table or share a couch with other classmates or even strangers. They might also be confused if people are coming and going to the library throughout the day.

During orientation and afterward, the librarian should make an attempt to get to know the child individually and to build a trusting relationship with him or her. The message should be made clear to the child that library staff are available to help and to listen. That personal connection is probably the most important part of any library introduction.

To help all users, not just youth with ASDs, librarians might consider creating voice-over and captioned presentations (e.g., PowerPoint) with images of the library facilities, resources, and staff. These presentations can be uploaded onto the library web portal for easy access from any location. Other step-by-step guides can also be uploaded onto this site for youth to download, print out, and study so they can feel comfortable and prepared when they visit the library.

EDUCATIONAL SETTINGS

By its very nature, school is both a structured and a semichaotic place. Daily schedules and time periods, assigned spaces, adult supervision, an established curriculum, rules, and expectations all lend order to the place. Nevertheless, that order differs from those that children with ASDs have experienced at home or in most other public places. Moreover, the other students in school can be very unpredictable and sometimes rigid or intolerant themselves. School is not an easy place for youth with ASDs to navigate. Nor is it easy for the school community to relate to youth with ASDs and figure out how to optimize their formal educational experiences.

Nevertheless, youth with ASDs benefit from attending school and participating with typical students. Research has repeatedly shown that youth with ASDs become more socially competent, have more friends and a supportive social network, and achieve more advanced individualized education program goals than their counterparts in segregated educational settings (Harrower and Dunlap 2001). Although mainstreamed students might not improve academically more than segregated students, they do not learn less. Furthermore, with years in mainstreamed education, youth with ASDs are more likely to be employable.

What are some of the behaviors that youth with ASDs may exhibit in school, particularly at the start or when under stress? It should be noted that these children may exhibit both extremes of the behavioral spectrum, which can be frustrating for others:

- anxiety, which may be exhibited through fidgeting, pacing, mumbling, or chewing
- withdrawn or reclusive behavior, or clinginess
- over- or underemotional reaction to situations
- tics or repetitive or unusual behaviors that may be socially inappropriate

However, when these students become more comfortable in their educational settings, they may have several skills and attributes that benefit the class:

- strong sense of fairness
- honesty and forthrightness
- advanced specialized ability in math, art, music, technology, or other areas
- advanced knowledge in areas of interest
- strong associative abilities in pattern recognition
- a presence that gives other students opportunities to learn about ASDs and improve their own social skills

In addition, having youth with ASDs in the classroom and library can motivate adults to be more organized and inclusive in their practices.

In any case, transitions between the home environment and school, and between school levels, are often the most difficult time for youth with ASDs. As general practice, educators and librarians should provide opportunities for these children to pilot test new environments in a controlled manner: when both the child and the site are calm and comfortable, and when the site has few people and little activity, so that staff can pay complete attention to the child. As mentioned already, providing a presentation document (e.g., binder, PowerPoint, video, podcast) is a way for the child, parents, and service providers to explain and discuss the new learning environment at home.

Preschool

In preschool everyone is on a somewhat even playing field. Hardly any child reads, understands phonemes or math, knows what school is like, or knows how to be social. Even though classmates may know that some of their peers have ASDs, they haven't been socialized enough to criticize or ostracize them.

However, even if children with ASDs have participated in intensive early interventions, mainstream preschool can be very disorienting for several reasons (Plimley, Bowen, and Morgan 2007):

- Many children congregate in the same, usually large, space.
- The atmosphere is often high energy and noisy.
- Children and adults may come and go, sometimes unpredictably. Some individuals may be present regularly, but others might attend sometimes.
- The space is likely to have lots of stimulating displays, learning corners, and so on.
- Children may have choices to make, such as activities and use of materials.
- Children are encouraged (and pressured) to participate and conform socially.
- Children are likely to be grouped in different ways at different times.

No wonder, then, that children with ASDs may enter preschool with anxiety, and even show regressive behavior. To mitigate such fears, parents can schedule visits before the school year begins and can help their child learn the classroom rules ahead of time. Preschool personnel can create and make available videotapes and photographs of the preschool in session and can preassign a class buddy. To help all children in preschool, preschool teachers can teach sharing skills, such as using a talking stick to signal who has the floor.

Elementary School

Elementary school extends the formal education day and poses new challenges for children with ASDs. In a certain way, the day is more structured, but children have to deal with much larger sets of youngsters at different ages in between class. The learning stakes are also higher, as grades and standardized tests—and their consequences—become part of the picture. Furthermore, children are less likely to get personal, one-on-one attention and differentiated instruction. Overall, the social norms become more constrained, certainly by age nine, when peer friendships become more important. Girls may find their nurturing gene and mother children with ASDs, whereas boys may shun them as a threat to their impending identities.

In elementary school libraries, students visit the library mainly as a class, which is probably easier for children with ASDs than going alone. Such library programs tend to focus on literacy: sharing a variety of materials, teaching how to handle materials, and promoting leisure literacy activities. Children with ASDs might have problems engaging with the material or might have trouble with some physical activities.

Some of the ways that teachers and librarians can help these children feel comfortable and engaged include the following:

- providing routines, be it for the day, a library visit, or procedures for doing activities
- getting to know all children's strengths and weaknesses, and interests and needs
- monitoring social interactions, and preventing and addressing inappropriate behaviors
- determining optimum seating
- creating learning stations for independent and small-group work

Middle School

Some educators contend that going from elementary to middle school is the hardest transition for youngsters, mainly because of the change to class periods, subject-specialist teachers, and more demanding coursework. Students tend to learn basic research processes and to do project work in the library.

Youth with ASDs have trouble transitioning from one task to another, and the stricter time frames of middle school can prove challenging for them. Having different teachers and classmates makes those transitions even harder. More substantial collaborative work is also expected in middle school, which can be challenging for all students as they need to negotiate roles, expectations, social norms, and work habits for each project.

Even with all those factors, probably the most difficult part of middle school is social life. During these critical years, the balance for finding approval shifts from adults to peers. Students at this age can be very cliquish and intolerant, and their allegiances can change overnight. Bullying occurs more at this age than at any other time. Social status and norms can be arbitrary, with appearance (both in body image and in dress) playing a significant factor. Trying to fit in is hard work for any middle schooler, but particularly for youth with ASDs. Even the most current magazines and the Internet cannot keep up with the social currents at any school.

Having a middle school point person and advocate, such as a counselor, is imperative to provide a stable adult figure in the school life of youth with ASDs. That person needs to participate in the preteen's support team and help optimize class schedules, classmates, and teacher assignments. Academic and social buddies can also help students with ASDs succeed in both arenas, and because some students will likely take the same set of courses, youth with ASDs can see some familiar faces throughout the day. In terms of social norms, classic clothes such as T-shirts and jeans are usually socially acceptable, and school uniforms can be a real godsend.

In the library, signs can help all students remember library procedures. School library collections should include accessible materials on academic and personal topics. Differentiated spaces for specific functions can help regulate sound levels and localize action. Providing earphones and "instant" table dividers can further cut down on distractions. At this age, some students can serve as library aides, with training on how to deal with different kinds of students, including those with ASDs. These aides can provide a stabling presence for their peers who have ASDs.

High School

High-stakes reality sets in during the high school years as grades determine postsecondary directions to a large extent. At the same time that academics are more rigorous, more self-management skills are expected, which is a core issue for youth with ASDs. The nature of the learning activities becomes more challenging for students with ASDs because they are expected to think abstractly, analytically, and creatively, which often does not play to their strengths. Teachers are more likely to lecture, and student work is more competitive, although collaboration on projects may occur. However, none of these trends is easy for youth with ASDs, particularly with having to deal with five or more subjects daily, each having its own "lens" or perspective on how to learn.

Depending on the school, some life skills and vocational training are offered, which can help these youth. In addition, physical education courses often teach lifelong fitness, such as swimming, dancing, golf, and even active gaming (i.e., simulated exercise and sports using technology such as Wii systems); such activities can seed leisure-time interests and help youth with ASDs in honing their body sense. If a student with an ASD has an individualized education program (IEP), transition planning to adulthood is required, so that he or she can get individualized help in workplace skills, social skills, independent living strategies, and guidance in self-determination.

As in middle school, youth with ASDs have to navigate the complexities of social life in high school. Besides the larger varying groups and spaces that youth with ASDs have to deal with, sexual activity is more prevalent at this age. As mentioned before, youth with ASDs are developing individuals first, so they are seeking close pals and romantic relationships. However, those increasingly complex social needs require accompanying social skills, which may be difficult for youth with ASDs to learn and for their parents to acknowledge and address; fortunately, most high schools teach these skills and the issues that accompany them. Now more than ever, youth with ASDs usually learn enough self-awareness to recognize that they differ from their classmates, which can lead to frustration and depression.

Simultaneously, developmental physiological changes can increase dysfunctional reactions to social challenges and personal needs for self-identity, so that some youth with ASDs—more often males—may act out aggressively and threateningly. Such behaviors can result in disciplinary action such as school suspension, which gives the student a time-out but can inadvertently lead to even more disruptive behavior as the student realizes that such acting out can result in more time to be alone and not have to deal with high school problems. School teams should preemptively teach youth with ASDs self-regulatory and coping skills, and should brainstorm appropriate disciplinary action that can redirect behavior into more positive channels.

High school is also more "porous" than middle school, meaning that outside issues come onto the campus more often: weekend activities, jobs, cars, consumerism, drugs, race issues, sexual orientation and life-style choices, religion, social activism. Options for taking risks increase significantly during these years, and youth with ASDs may feel overwhelmed. Cocurricular and service clubs sponsored by schools, libraries, or other youth-serving agencies provide healthy outlets for these issues and serve as a way for youth with ASDs to find like-minded peers to strengthen their social supports. Especially because youth with ASDs are likely to have social friends and to participate in social activities, youth-serving agencies should proactively seek ways to invite them to participate, probably through their service teams.

High school libraries can provide the same kinds of resources and services as in middle school libraries. In addition, high-functioning youth with ASDs may be good candidates for library aides as technicians, shelvers, art helpers, and processors. Youth with ASDs can receive individual training that matches their strengths, and they can learn good workplace habits in the process. Social stories and other learning aids such as videos and reference sheets can reinforce library procedures, and as youth with ASDs become experts, they can make good trainers for beginning library aides. Such positive experiences can lead to postsecondary education and careers.

LEARNING ISSUES

All children learn but not in the same way or about the same things. Learning preferences are shaped by biology, environmental factors, prior experience (both good and bad), situations, and culture, among other things. As mentioned already, children with ASDs have unique learning characteristics, not only because ASDs and their manifestations vary widely but also because each child must negotiate how to deal with these variations. Nonetheless, certain learning tendencies are evidenced among most youth with autism, so librarians and other educators can at least start with some basic assumptions, which they can then test for their validity and adjust accordingly. Youth with ASDs tend to:

- prefer to learn by trial and error rather than observation
- prefer constructive play over symbolic play
- use language to request something rather than to comment on something (the latter reflects an emotional social exchange)
- have difficulty imitating motor actions
- prefer static rather than transient information (e.g., still images rather than moving images, text rather than oral content)
- think associatively rather than sequentially

Specific learning differences arise in the different categories of ASDs. In the United States, the educational system has its own norms and expectations, which do not always align well with the preferences of students with ASDs. Therefore, librarians need to make learning more inclusive and to draw on the skills of youth with ASDs (Spiegel 2003).

Social Learning Disabilities
The following are some social learning disabilities that youth with ASDs may display, along with interventions, noted in italic, that service providers may use to help a person with an ASD:

Lack of awareness of others: fails to see what is happening in the class, which affects learning. *Motivate the child through connections to personal interests and self-satisfaction.*

Lack of social and emotional reciprocity: does not show empathy in ways that help direct interaction, which minimizes the impact of approval from adults as motivation. *Validate the student's self-esteem and competency.*

Lack of social imitation: does not seem to be motivated to copy other's actions or attitudes, which minimizes the effect of teaching by modeling. *Do not use peer pressure.*

Communication Learning Disabilities

The following are some communication learning disabilities that youth with ASDs may show, and interventions, noted in italic, that service providers can use to help a person with an ASD:

Poor ability to comprehend and use facial expressions of gestures: misses visual cues to linguistic intent; does not express comprehension through gesture or expression, so educators may underestimate child's understanding. *Use other means for the child to indicate understanding (e.g., prompting a direct signal, referring to a picture-card communication system).*

Difficulty understanding spoken language: may have selective listening depending on topic. *Use visual cues, emphasize nouns, and take into consideration the context of the topic.*

Difficulty using spoken language: language may be echolalic, very concise, or monotone; uses language to meet a personal need rather than to share information, which impedes collaboration. *Leverage echolalia to rehearse meaning, incorporate choral reading and poetry, and encourage expressive language to share information about high-interest topics.*

Restrictive or Repetitive Learning Disabilities

The following are some restrictive or repetitive learning disabilities that youth with ASDs may experience; interventions are noted in italic:

Lack of imaginative play: thinks literally and shows limited representation of play situations, which minimizes opportunities for practicing social rules or associating actions with verbal expression. *Start with acting out or simulating real situations concretely, then transition to hypothetical situations; simulate highly motivational situations.*

Limited, repetitive interests: avoids novel objects and actions, and lacks curiosity, which impedes learning through exploration. *Consider repetitive activity as downtime, a break from learning; introduce novel topics and objects under low-stress conditions; watch for signs of boredom to introduce novelty or surprise; and link comfortable items with new situations.*

Several general strategies can set up the conditions that facilitate overall communication and improve communication skills, starting with setting up the environment to motivate youth to communicate, such as by displaying interesting materials to request, requiring youth to share needed objects and supplies, and requiring verbal communication as part of ongoing routines such as passing papers.

Augmentative and alternative communication systems can also be used, such as communication partners (e.g., a friend who understands a child with ASD better than others), visual collections of objects and actions, and the Picture Exchange Communication System (which can be used, for example, to request items, to discriminate among items, to help build and extend sentence structure, and to comment on objects or actions in the environment). The brand PECS is one example of a visually based system that uses small picture cards to represent something that the child wants to have or do, such as a banana or to play with a favorite toy. The child gives the specific card to a person at the desired time; this action constitutes a request.

In any case, librarians should acknowledge communication attempts and reinforce meaning by rephrasing the expression, similarly to the way that adults help young children talk. Adults can also elaborate on what the child is saying, which can help sustain the interaction and complexity of the conversation.

WHAT HELPS YOUTH WITH ASDs LEARN?

Ranae Mathias, mother of a teen with autism, was once asked in an informal interview, "How does your son learn?" She replied:

> My son and I talked about it, but he said he doesn't know how he learns. I can tell you that he learns visually. When he learned to read, he memorized the words (only took once) and then he could read them. Never could sound anything out; phonics was a mystery to him. Math is very difficult. Again, he memorized his basic facts and spelling words easily and can recall them, but when doing any computation he struggles. He made it through basic algebra in special ed classes but hasn't taken math now his senior year. He took a

very long time to learn to tell time and read a calendar. In short, if it is an abstract concept, he really has a hard time grasping it. If he can memorize it or learn it visually, he has more success. We live in a very crazy, hilly town with streets that wind every which way and connect back up again. He has been able to navigate his way through town since he was about three (again, visual memory). So, his main strength is visual memory skills. Fine motor skills such as handwriting are difficult for him. He does type but not in a formal manner (neither does his mother!).

After reading this chapter, it may seem that mainstream education is not ready for youth with ASDs, and vice versa. However, inclusive education provides useful and enlightening experiences for everyone. Furthermore, the message about the uniqueness of each person with an ASD—as well as everyone else—should be clear by now. In summary, getting to know young people on an individual basis, learning about their wants and needs, promoting mutual respect and support, and challenging them to progress are good practices for any kind of education and human endeavor in general. The Wisconsin Assistive Technology Initiative (2009) developed a useful, thorough assessment instrument for K–12 educators to gather data in order to identify specific areas of needs and to develop technology supports for students with ASDs. Also, the more librarians and other educators know about ASDs, the more effective they can be.

Nevertheless, educational challenges inevitably occur. Here are a few techniques to make the educational journey a little less bumpy for everyone:

- Provide a safe, supportive environment with clear, consistent, and fair expectations and directions.
- Provide schedules, and prepare everyone for transitions.
- Try to meet children at their level of comprehension and comfort. Modify or make adjustments in interactions accordingly, such as changing pace, changing sound level and pitch, using simpler and more concrete words, providing more or less stimulatory input, breaking down processes into smaller steps, and providing visual clues. If one approach doesn't work, then try something else.

- Identify possible triggers of inappropriate behavior, and try to avoid or mitigate them. A useful strategy is to agree on a signal to use when an inappropriate behavior begins or when the child starts feeling stressed, so that both parties can become aware and self-correct without public embarrassment.
- Figure out the reason for inappropriate behavior, and try to work with the child to find more socially acceptable ways for the child to attain that goal.
- Monitor behaviors. Unless safety is a concern, introduce interventions incrementally. At the first encounter, ignoring or redirecting the behavior may suffice. Use positive reinforcement to teach skills, and reinforce desired action immediately after it occurs, at least when first teaching a skill. Try to replace a negative activity with a more motivating and enjoyable activity.
- Don't expect a child to be reasonable or take positive action during a meltdown. Focus on helping the child calm down and regain equilibrium before indicating what he or she should do.
- Provide break time and downtime as needed.
- Encourage peer help and support.
- Realize that no one is perfect, and that you can't win them all.
- Be patient with others and with yourself.

REFERENCES

Harrower, J., and G. Dunlap. "Including Children with Autism in General Education Classrooms: A Review of Effective Strategies." *Behavior Modification* 25 (2001): 762–84.

Plimley, L., M. Bowen, and H. Morgan. *Autistic Spectrum Disorders in the Early Years*. London: Paul Chapman, 2007.

Spiegel, B. *Helping Children with Autism Learn*. New York: Oxford University Press, 2003.

Wisconsin Assistive Technology Initiative. *Assistive Technology Supports for Individuals with Autism Spectrum Disorder*. Milton: Wisconsin Assistive Technology Initiative, 2009. www.wati.org/content/supports/free/pdf/ASDManual-1.pdf.

CHAPTER 2

Team Management Approach

T HE PHRASE "IT TAKES A VILLAGE TO RAISE A CHILD" APPLIES TO ALL children, but also to youth with ASDs. Because the causes, manifestations, and impact of autism spectrum disorder vary among children, it takes the unique perspectives of several specialists to assess the situation and offer effective suggestions. Furthermore, because youth with ASDs often have troubles interacting with their environment, be it for academic or social reasons, the more that the people around them can understand the dynamics, the easier it is for others to help. By knowing and understanding an individual's current status, others can help him or her deal with those realities and change some of the conditions of their interactions.

TEAM MEMBER CONTRIBUTIONS

Throughout the lifetime of a person with ASDs, a number of service providers can provide valuable support, from the parents and pediatrician to transition counselors and social benefits experts. When these experts can inform one another and work collaboratively in support of a person with ASDs, the resultant team can maximize positive impact.

Each team member brings a unique perspective and set of skills that can support and help youth with ASDs.

Youth with ASDs

The most important, most consistent team member is the youth with an ASD him- or herself. Even though many youth might not be very self-aware, particularly as children, they have to live with themselves and experience their own successes and frustrations. Even at a young age, people can often tell when someone is talking about them, if by no other sign than tone of voice or body language. It makes sense, and is respectful, to treat children as team members and to interact with them in terms of planning and assessment. As children develop, they gain insight and social consciousness, and they can bring that awareness to the table. Also, children are likely to communicate stress, engagement, and calm, which are very important things that other team members can draw on. High-functioning teens can take pride in participating in transition planning, and they are more likely to succeed if they can communicate their interests and needs to the rest of the team and test out alternative scenarios.

Parents and Guardians

Second to the child, parents and guardians of a child with ASDs are the most involved and invested. With their life experience, especially if they have other children, they are the most informed about their child's development, capabilities, interests, and needs; as such, they serve as the child's representative. They are also in the best position to determine whether a certain team member is a good fit for the child. Parents and guardians are also the most likely to reinforce the implementation of treatment plans in multiple settings. Parents are the child's first and continuing teachers, role models, and advocates; they need to have or gain the skills to help their child succeed throughout life.

Educators

Educators bring to the team their content knowledge and experience with youth. They may also have prior knowledge about and experience with ASDs. Educators routinely communicate with students and families, so they can inform parents about their child's behavior and learning, and they can gain information about the child's behaviors at home—thus bridging school and home life and providing a seamless support system. Furthermore, most teachers help students learn skills for use in daily life, not just the next course at school. As part of the school and local community, educators might know about local resources or experts who can help the child in other aspects of life. In terms of needs for assistance, educators can help youth in selecting and experimenting with appropriate accommodations, such as recording class lectures and getting extended time when taking a test.

Special Education Personnel

Special education personnel vary greatly in expertise and function, from teacher aides to administrators, with line staff focusing on pathology, therapy, and specific disabilities, including ASDs. For example, the California State Department of Education (2009) has a specific class authorization for teaching students with ASDs, which requires that such teachers be able to identify characteristics of students with ASDs and their core challenges; implement data-based, multifaceted strategies to engage and instruct students with ASDs; and collaborate as a multidisciplinary team member, including with community service providers.

In contrast, aides usually do not teach but serve more as facilitators or supporters, helping children who cannot perform independently and facilitating action. In some cases, aides act as "shadows," helping the child to pay attention to teachers and peers. Aides usually have some special education training, but they might not be autism experts or have theory-based preparation. Therefore, aides should meet regularly with autism specialists.

All special education staff need to understand the characteristics and development of youth with special needs, including those with ASDs; be able to assess and teach (or assist teaching) them; and collaborate with the school community to help them succeed.

Counselors

According to the American School Counselor Association (2005), counselors deal with individuals' academic career, social, and personal needs. They function in four domains: guidance on curriculum and activities, individual assessment and planning, responsive services, and system support. They also advocate for individuals at review sessions, such as for IEPs. Their skills can guide youth with ASDs along several dimensions and help them coordinate academic and social behaviors.

School Psychologists

School psychologists address issues of personal behavior, social development and adjustment, and academic difficulties (National Association of School Psychologists 2003). They develop prevention programs, assess youth development, and recommend interventions. One of their strengths is data-driven decision making and accountability, which benefits the entire team.

School Social Workers

School social workers bridge home, school, and community in assessing factors that affect learning, emotional health, and social adjustment (U.S. Bureau of Labor Statistics 2012). They work with adults to support youth with ASDs through training, providing intervention strategies, and coordinating community resources. They also deal with some of the darker issues that can jeopardize youth, such as truancy, foster care, and teen pregnancy.

Clinical and Rehabilitation Specialists

Several specialists provide focused interventions for youth with ASDs (Council for Exceptional Children 2011).

Speech-language pathologists diagnose and recommend interventions for speech disorders (e.g., voice, articulation, fluency), delayed language, and language disorders of aphasia (lost speech or language ability), any of which can manifest in youth with ASDs.

Occupational therapists help youth with ASDs perform tasks in different settings by assisting them in improving motor functions and reasoning abilities, to compensate for function loss.

Physical therapists provide services that help restore function, improve mobility, and prevent or limit physical disabilities of youth with ASDs.

Kinesiotherapists apply exercise principles to improve the mobility, endurance, and strength of individuals with functional limitations.

School Nurses

School nurses focus on students' health and development. They assess the youth's health-related condition, recommend and provide health maintenance plans, implement health education, counsel families, and connect families with community health services (U.S. Bureau of Labor Statistics 2012). Youth with ASDs often have health issues, so nurses are a valuable resource on the team.

Reading Specialists

Reading specialists and literacy coaches have advanced training in reading assessment and interventions. They collaborate with the school community as reading resource consultants, and they conduct trainings for team members on reading issues. They support classroom teachers and offer pullout instruction for developmentally appropriate remediation. They can play a central role in helping diagnose and address language issues in youth with ASDs and, working with other school community members, in consistently applying appropriate strategies.

Technology Specialists

Technology specialists oversee the smooth operation of computer-based technology, be it for instructional or administrative use. Some staff focus on installation and maintenance issues, and others also help with curriculum integration issues. Technology specialists can also facilitate participation by youth with ASDs in technology activities. Assistive technology specialists assess needs and recommend appropriate technologies. They also help acquire and maintain technology, and they can train youth with ASDs and service providers in how to use the technology.

Activities Personnel

Activities personnel, such as coaches, spirit directors, and performance teachers, oversee cocurricular activities, which can support specific interests of youth with ASDs and provide opportunities for developing social skills. Activities directors plan, supervise, and assess activity programs, and they work with school and community members. They can identify possible areas of interest for youth with ASDs and facilitate training of relevant staff to provide effective support to youth.

Administrators

Administrators are responsible for keeping education operational; they lead people and manage things. The National Association of Elementary School Principals (2001) identified twelve areas of responsibility for administrators, all of which affect youth with ASDs and their treatment team:

1. Contact and supervise staff: monitor staff relative to meeting the needs of youth with ASDs.
2. Interact with students: develop professional relations with youth with ASDs.
3. Student management and discipline: make sure that youth with ASDs are treated respectfully and that youth with ASDs are appropriately disciplined.
4. Contact community and parents: serve on and facilitate IEP teams, network with community service providers, and provide training and support for parents.
5. Interact with central office staff: facilitate paperwork and other clerical functions that affect youth with ASDs.
6. Curriculum development: ensure that youth with ASDs receive a full education, including social and life skills.
7. Staff development: facilitate training about youth with ASDs and how to support them.
8. Student placement and evaluation: serve on IEP teams and facilitate appropriate student transition placements.
9. Facilities management: ensure that youth with ASDs have appropriate furniture and distraction-free spaces.
10. Budget management: locate and allocate funds to support the education of youth with ASDs.
11. Safety and security issues: ensure that youth with ASDs are safe and do not wander off-campus.
12. Other duties as assigned: manage crises that affect youth with ASDs.

Librarians

As part of a treatment team, librarians have the expertise and experience to help the team in several ways, including the following:

- evaluating and organizing relevant resources for youth with ASDs and their service providers
- helping families provide an effective learning environment and choose appropriate resources for their children
- locating community resources to support youth with ASDs
- researching best practices relative to ASDs
- spearheading knowledge management by developing databases, wikis, and other means to collect, organize, retrieve, and share team information
- training youth with ASDs, team members, and other school community members in the use and incorporation of technology, including assistive technology
- training youth with ASDs to work as library and technology aides
- participating in action research to optimize interventions for youth with ASDs
- collaborating with the school and larger community to advocate for and support youth with ASDs

By working with the treatment team, librarians can also learn effective ways to work with and support youth with ASDs. Be they in public or school settings, librarians can observe how team members and youth interact and work together effectively. Librarians can also learn effective strategies to help these youth improve their cognitive and social skills.

COORDINATED SERVICE TEAMS

The team members share the same overarching goal: to help the young person with an ASD to fulfill his or her potential to the greatest degree possible. To that end, the team looks at several elements:

- What the reality is of the young person: day-to-day life, personal and social acceptance, and unique characteristics of the person
- What challenges the young person faces because of the ASD: loss of possibilities, differences from typical peers, possible stigma or prejudice that might arise because of the disorder

- What are potentialities for the young person: explanation of the disorder and possible basis, possible outcomes, treatments, individuals who can assume responsibility for the outcome

The team is responsible for assessing the young person with ASD and developing plans that will help and support that young person. As the team does this work, the members should consider several factors (Plimley, Bowen, and Morgan 2007):

- the youth's receptive and expressive language in different settings and situations
- the youth's gross and fine motor coordination, including aspects of use of space, play, academics, and articulation
- the youth's academic and cognitive skills, rote and generative skills, subject interests, and group work
- the youth's personal and social skills, including life skills in different settings and situations, as well as personality traits
- effective and ineffective prior interventions

For teams to act effectively, certain behaviors need to be in place (Plimley, Bowen, and Morgan 2007):

- mutual tolerance and respect as individuals
- understanding and respect for each person's expertise and role, and overlap or complements with one another
- willingness and commitment to communicate and work with one another on the behalf of the youth with ASDs
- honest and realistic approach
- listening skills
- flexibility
- positive communication and encouragement of strengths

Some treatment programs need highly collaborative teams. One such program is applied behavior analysis (ABA), a systematic behavior-modification process that can be used at home and, to a degree, in schools. This treatment involves breaking down tasks into small achievable steps, each of which builds on the previous one. Each action is documented, and the team uses the documentation to guide teaching and rewards, called reinforcers, which are given for correct responses. Because ABA requires consistent behavior across settings, the entire team needs to apply the same reinforcers. The teacher who coordinates the program may be a senior therapist or a case manager, both of whom have less educational experience than most classroom teachers. However, classroom teachers need training on ASDs and specific training in ABA. Other specialists provide unique expertise for specific aspects of the process, such as resource specialists, school psychologists, and speech therapists; they can work with the students on a one-on-one basis while another team member adapts the curriculum for group engagement. Because ABA fine-tunes a child's behavior and interventions on the basis of close observation and analysis, it is imperative for team members to inform one another about the specific reinforcers and the child's progress. The child benefits from this consistent and intensive treatment, which is optimized by teamwork. When team members differ in their analysis or treatment, the child receives a mixed message, which undermines the structure of ABA treatment. Each person has to respect the unique roles of teammates and work to smooth out differences to help the child. An ABA program can also exist on a schoolwide basis. For example, a school-based ABA program can help case managers and program managers optimize travel for youth with ASDs, including removing the need for youth to walk through unknown or possibly unsafe neighborhoods. Furthermore, a school-based ABA program facilitates communication and coordination among team members.

Even when constant assessment, monitoring, and close collaboration are not called for, the team supporting a youth with an ASD needs to plan collaboratively and communicate regularly. An individualized education program (IEP) provides a standardized framework in which to design appropriate treatments. The following IEP is a representative sample for a high schooler with an ASD.

INDIVIDUALIZED EDUCATION PROGRAM

Name of student: __Jeffrey Xavier__   Age: _17_   Gender: _Male_

School District ID #: __000-000-000__   Eligibility: _Autism_

Date of IEP: __06/12/2011__   Type of IEP: _Annual_

Grade: _12_ Ethnicity: _Latino_ School of Attendance: _ABC High School_

Parent information: __Ada Xavier__   Phone: _(000) 000-0000_

Home address: __123 A Street, Long Beach, CA 90815__

Date of initial IEP: __05/23/1998__

TEAM MEMBERS
The following team members were present at this meeting:

Name (print)	Signature	Role
Ada Xavier	*Ada Xavier*	Participant
Shelley Smith	*Shelley Smith*	Teacher, special ed
Deborah Chase	*Deborah Chase*	Administrative designee
Jeff Xavier	*Jeff Xavier*	Student
Tina Arora	*Tina Arora*	Advocate
Hilda Rhodes	*Hilda Rhodes*	Teacher, gen ed

INFORMED CONSENT FOR PLACEMENT IN SPECIAL EDUCATION

☒ I have been given a copy of the IEP Process & Parent/Guardian Rights brochure.

☒ I accept this Individualized Educational Plan.

ASSESSMENT OF PREVIOUS IEP GOALS

Goals pertain to the period 6/13/2012 to 6/12/2013

Assessment of goal pertaining to speech/language skills

GOAL 1: Jeffrey will answer questions beginning with *wh* (i.e., what, why, when, and where) pertaining to short stories with 90 percent accuracy, four to five times in different settings.

CURRENT PERFORMANCE: Jeffrey is able to answer most questions when provided with moderate prompts. Restatement of the question is required two to three times.

GROWTH: Did the student demonstrate growth or advancement in the last year?

☐ Yes, accomplished the goal

☒ No, did not meet the goal but demonstrated some advancement (70 percent accuracy, 2/5 times)

☐ No advancement observed

LEVEL OF INDEPENDENCE: Does the student demonstrate a higher level of independence as related to the goal?

☒ greater independence

☐ no change in independence

☐ lower independence

Should the goal be discontinued?

☐ no further needs related to the goal

☒ continue goal

Assessment of goal pertaining to career development:

GOAL 2: With minimal prompts, Jeffrey will identify correct bus route to take, identify correct stop by pushing button or telling staff or bus driver with 80 percent accuracy, four to five times a week.

CURRENT PERFORMANCE: With minimal prompts, Jeffrey can identify correct bus route to take, identify correct stop by pushing button or telling staff or bus driver with 100 percent accuracy four to five times a week.

DEVELOPMENTAL TEAM FUNCTIONS

At each point in life, the team changes to some degree because of different bases for services and normal personnel transitions. Although such changes are supposed to improve conditions, the act of change itself can be frustrating for both the person with ASDs and the important people in his or her life. The service team members have to readjust to one another while maintaining ongoing support for the person with an ASD. Without strong communication and coordination, team members might counteract one another's assessment and treatment, which not only confuses the person with ASD but also can negatively affect his or her situation. Such changes in personnel are another reason some people with ASDs live with family members as adults; a consistent service provider is a key factor in successful daily life.

Early Childhood

Autism spectrum disorders are either congenital or appear as a regressive onset by age three. Typically, a parent or guardian sees developmental delays in the child and asks for a screening by a pediatrician. A brief assessment can then determine whether a more in-depth diagnosis makes sense. At that point, several specialists may come into play:

- developmental physician
- behavioral physician
- neurologist to focus on brain development
- speech-language pathologist to focus on language-based activities
- audiologist to focus on hearing issues
- psychologist
- physical therapist
- behavior analyst
- occupational therapist
- social worker
- educator

These people all interact with the child and his or her family, with the primary pediatrician serving as the professional point person, at least in the beginning. All of these people look at the child's current and past medical condition, symptom history, developmental history, sensorimotor history, and family history. Together, they can put together the pieces to get a rich picture of the child and his or her situation (Robinson 2011). The result is a formal diagnosis, which includes the following:

- individual profile noting social-emotional development, sensorimotor profile, and intelligence determination
- medical concerns noting general health and health maintenance (e.g., diet)
- medical associations such as a seizure disorder, immunologic diseases, and metabolic variations
- ASD target symptoms that require treatment
- family systems and resources
- community opportunities such as public developmental services and local outreach organizations

From this diagnosis, a treatment plan is developed, and team members are identified to help in the child's development. From birth to age three, this plan usually takes the form of an individualized family service plan (IFSP); later, school districts can use an IFSP for children with disabilities between the ages of three and five. An IFSP states the child's functional abilities in the areas of physical, cognitive, communication, social-emotional, and adaptive development. Typically, the plan prioritizes the action in terms of immediate need and paced time frames, and it notes the criteria and procedures for determining progress in meeting outcomes. The plan can be quite complex, building on intensive home environment treatment that weaves together relationship interactions, speech therapy, occupational therapy, and education. The IFSP also addresses issues of scheduling, medications, finances, and family emotional support.

It is at this point that each member of the team needs to align with the child's personality; because the plan itself is the result of highly individualized facets, the service providers need to coalesce their attitudes. Coordinated team management needs to be established by a professional, ideally by a pediatrician. If an IFSP is not used, parents can manage the program with support from professionals. The team manager collects ongoing data about the child and keeps each member informed of the treatment and its impact, particularly with quarterly reviews of the IFSP. When team members leave, before doing so, they should train the new member to ensure consistency and accuracy in the directives of the treatment plan.

School Settings

School-age children transition to an academic-centric individualized education program (IEP) and its accompanying team. As with the IFSP, IEPs are developed with a team of service providers and the family. In addition to the team that participates in early childhood assessment, the following people may be involved (required personnel are noted by an asterisk) in an IEP team:

- special education staff: professionals (at least one)* and para-educators or aides
- classroom teachers (at least one)*
- school librarians
- other service support personnel, such as reading specialists, technology specialists, pupil support specialists (e.g., academic and personal counselors, school psychologists, school social workers), and school health specialists

- administrators, including district personnel (one district representative)* in charge of special education funding
- parents (at least one)*

Usually, when a child transitions from an IFSP to an IEP, the team manager also changes, as school districts often assign a teacher or a licensed staff member. That manager then coordinates communication and assessment among home, school, and other agencies. Furthermore, prior plans should be passed on to the new team members to ensure continuity.

The main challenge for the team manager is to involve the rest of the school community who are not part of the plan but may well be affected by it, such as the school librarian. Not only should other teachers and support personnel be informed, they may have experiences and insights that will improve the IEP.

Transition to Adulthood

Another key transition point is during adolescence, at the brink of adulthood, when a youth with an ASD ends secondary education (for the legal requirements and beneficial practices during this transition, see Wall 2007). Five transition areas must be assessed and addressed annually during this phase: home living, recreation and leisure, community participation (e.g., transportation, clubs, social agencies, civic activities), postsecondary education and training, and employment. By the time a youth with ASD is about fourteen, his or her IEP should address preparation for these transitions. As in the earlier stages of an IEP, several people are involved: an administrator, a special education teacher, and an appropriate regular classroom teacher. Obviously, the youth and a parent must be invited to the meeting, as should a member of the assessment team. When exploring college or postsecondary education, a counselor and personnel from rehabilitation and social services should be present to explain options for the youth and to determine which postsecondary placements are most appropriate. Other people who might be involved at this time include physicians, mental health counselors, county case managers, Social Security personnel, and parole officers. More difficult to find are team members who can help youth develop recreational and leisure skills, manage a budget, make friends, and plan personal health care; in some areas, postsecondary institutions provide transition training—including life skills—for youth with special needs, including youth with ASDs, who would be grouped with a wide range of other young adults. In addition, the transition team should focus on the future as well as address a student's academic deficits.

The transition planning team manager is likely to be a classroom or special education teacher. The manager is in charge of inviting experts from outside the school and clarifying their roles at the meetings and in the plan. Sometimes the team manager contacts supporting agencies to help identify appropriate people to take part on the team. In this way, librarians can serve a useful role in helping locate relevant agencies. Just as the school-based IEP has a broader focus than the IFSP, the transition plan expands its scope to the community at large, which makes it even harder to schedule meetings and manage the team. Fortunately, technology such as email, online chat, and private wikis can facilitate in establishing a resource list of support and in organizing ongoing data collection and analysis. In most cases, youth with ASDs should participate in these communications for several reasons: they are the most informed about what they experience and need, they can gain social skills, and they can become better prepared to accept change.

As part of the transition program, the team members look at adult programs for youth with ASDs, some of which are quite comprehensive, providing both employment and housing. Although families and youth usually visit the institutions that offer these programs, it makes sense for other team members to suggest good questions for youth and their families to ask, and to accompany them in order to provide their perspective, as they all help youth with ASDs plan for their postsecondary futures. When families explore these programs, they should record or photograph the sites and inform the rest of the team about their experiences and feelings about the programs. Similarly, team members may belong to local networks that can identify community resources that would be a good match for a particular individual. Additionally, team members can serve as advocates for youth with ASDs, both for the individual with whom they are working and for youth with ASDs in general. As each person with an ASD transitions successfully into his or her community, that person lays the groundwork for others to follow.

REFERENCES

American School Counselor Association. *ASCA National Model.* Alexandria, VA: American School Counselor Association, 2005.

California State Department of Education. *New Special Education Added Authorizations.* Sacramento: California State Department of Education, 2009.

Council for Exceptional Children. SpecialEdCareers.org. Arlington, VA: Council for Exceptional Children, 2011.

National Association of Elementary School Principals. *Leading Learning Communities: Standards for What Principals Should Know and Be Able to Do.* Alexandria, VA: National Association of Elementary School Principals, 2001.

National Association of School Psychologists. *School Psychology: A Career That Makes a Difference.* Bethesda, MD: National Association of School Psychologists, 2003.

Plimley, L., M. Bowen, and H. Morgan. *Autistic Spectrum Disorders in the Early Years.* London: Paul Chapman, 2007.

Robinson, R. *Autism Solutions.* Don Mills, ON: Harlequin, 2011.

U.S. Bureau of Labor Statistics. *Occupational Outlook Handbook.* Washington, DC: U.S. Department of Labor, 2012.

Wall, K. *Education and Care for Adolescents and Adults with Autism: A Guide for Professionals and Carers.* Thousand Oaks, CA: Sage Publications, 2007.

CHAPTER 3

Inclusion and Universal Design in Libraries

LIBRARIES TRY TO PRACTICE INCLUSION: THEY SERVE ALL KINDS OF PEO-ple and strive to respond to and meet their various needs. For that reason, libraries try to have rich collections and adaptable services. Taking the approach of universal design, whereby material and digital resources are made physically and intellectually accessible to all users, including those with special needs, library programs should be accessible to all youth, including those with ASDs. This chapter covers some of the regulations that mandate equitable access and use. It then details how universal design applies to library facilities, selection and use of resources, interaction, and learning activities.

AN OVERVIEW OF INCLUSION
AND UNIVERSAL DESIGN

A basic tenet of libraries is free and equitable access to information. Libraries offer a neutral, safe learning space with resources and services available to all. Today's libraries expand that notion as they offer free access to computers, databases, and worldwide resources. However, libraries' ability to facilitate the use of these resources has been less even.

The central notion of inclusion is that communities benefit from diversity because people can have a wider basis from which to choose and use information. Interaction with different kinds of people exposes others to new ideas and practices, and it can increase mutual support. In terms of youth with ASDs, inclusion means that they have the right to participate, and benefit from participation, in typical community settings such as libraries where children without disabilities also participate.

For libraries, inclusion tends to focus on physical and intellectual access. Libraries should provide a rich collection of resources that meets users' diverse interests and needs. What materials can engage youth with ASDs? Are materials available at the reading level needed for their successful comprehension? What assistive technology targets this population? What accommodations in the library will help youth with ASDs use library resources, such as carrels to block off distractions?

Likewise, librarians need to think about services that will help youth with ASDs comprehend and use information effectively. How can library staff interact positively with these youth? What kind of instruction will engage them? Do library staff have access to IEPs, or do they work with other service providers, to know how to differentiate instruction?

A major element of inclusion is universal design: the design of strategies that enable all people to use products and environments without modification. In section 3(19) of the Assistive Technology Act of 1998, universal design was defined as a concept or philosophy for designing and delivering products and services that are usable by people with the widest possible range of functional capabilities, which include products and services that are directly usable (without requiring assistive technologies) and products and services that are made usable with assistive technologies.

The Center for Universal Design (1997) has identified seven guidelines to optimize usability and performance:

1. Equitable use
2. Flexibility in use
3. Simple, intuitive use, regardless of experience or language
4. Perceptible information that communicates necessary information regardless of ambient conditions or the user's sensory abilities
5. Tolerance for error and compensation for accidental or unintended action
6. Low physical effort that does not fatigue the user
7. Appropriate size and space for approach and use

The Center for Applied Special Technology (www.cast.org/library/UDLguidelines) clusters these principles of universal design for learning into three components: multiple means of representation, multiple means of engagement, and multiple means of expression. Universal design, therefore, uses a more intentional approach than inclusion, positing that one should proactively anticipate and address needs.

Hernon and Calvert (2006) applied universal design to libraries in educational settings, which can encompass populations of youth with ASDs:

1. Use accessible methods, such as web pages that comply with the Americans with Disabilities Act (ADA).
2. Allow youth to choose ways to demonstrate their competence.
3. Keep processes simple.
4. Use formats that can be accessed in different ways.
5. Anticipate differences in learning pace.
6. Use methods that minimize physical effort.
7. Provide flexible seating arrangements.
8. Encourage positive communication.
9. Maintain a positive learning environment of respect and high expectations.

The authors also gave specific suggestions for ways that libraries can implement universal design, such as using key-served software on networks to keep down licensing costs, sharing resources, partnering with other agencies for professional development, and ensuring that facility modifications are ADA compliant.

Working in the field of differentiated instruction, Tomlinson (1999) suggested the metaphor of an equalizer for describing supports and choices for students in universal-designed learning environments. Tomlinson also used the metaphor of a slider control to represent the scale of responses for nine academic factors:

1. Information, ideas, resources: from foundational to transformational
2. Knowledge representation: from concrete to abstract
3. Resources, issues, skills, goals: from simple to complex
4. Curriculum and developmental stages: from single facet to multiple facets
5. Insight, transfer, application: from small leap to large leap
6. Approaches, solutions, decisions: from more structured to more open
7. In process and products: from clearly defined problems to fuzzy problems
8. Planning and monitoring: from less independence to greater independence
9. Learning pace: from slow to quick

Inclusion and universal design are reasonable expectations of libraries in general, and they certainly apply to practices that address the needs and interests of youth with ASDs.

THE LAW AND AUTISM SPECTRUM DISORDERS

As advocates for their constituents, librarians should be aware of the legal bases for providing services to youth with autism. Some laws and legal decisions focus on K–12 settings, but most apply to all settings. Although some state-level legislation exists, federal mandates tend to drive most laws that affect the provision of services for this population.

History

The U.S. federal laws and legal decisions that apply to youth with autism predate the formal definition of autism. The first explicit mention of autism in the law was made in 1954, and several actions have occurred since then.

The 1954 Supreme Court case *Brown v. Board of Education* (347 U.S. 483 (1954)) ended the concept of separate-but-equal education. Although the intent of the case was race based, its implications affected special education. Students with special needs were typically assigned to a separate track of education, which could be located at a different site. This kind of separate education limited the opportunity for students with ASDs to interact with other students. As a result of the *Brown* decision, students with ASDs are more likely to experience their education at the same place as typical students, although they might be assigned a separate classroom in many cases.

A 1972 Supreme Court case pitted the Pennsylvania Association for Retarded Citizens against the commonwealth of Pennsylvania (343 Fed. Supp. 279 (1972)). In the same year, a similar case, *Mills v. Board of Education* (348 F. Supp. 866 (1972)) addressed a broad spectrum of children with disabilities. The result of the case was the mandate for a free public education program appropriate to each child's capacity. No longer could all special education students fall under a monolithic category, with one educational program for all of them. The law also stipulated that students should have an education that most approximates mainstream education. These cases laid the groundwork for the 1975 Education for All Handicapped Children Act (Pub. L. No. 94-142), which provided for free appropriate public education, including special education to meet the needs of all children with disabilities.

It should be noted that an earlier act, the 1973 Rehabilitation Act (Pub. L. No. 93-112), section 504, stated that exclusion from any educational program or activity based on disability constituted discrimination. Section 504 of the Rehabilitation Act required all children with disabilities to be educated in the least restrictive environment. In this act, which was amended in 1998, disabilities were defined as (1) a physical or mental impairment that substantially limits one or more major life activities or (2) a record of such an impairment, or being regarded as having such an impairment; individuals not qualified under the act may qualify for special services and accommodations under section 504.

The 1982 Supreme Court case *Board of Education v. Rowley* (458 U.S. 176 (1982)) addressed the quality of education that should be provided to students with special needs. The court determined that schools need to provide appropriate educational experiences for students with special needs, but they do not have to offer the *best* services. The intent behind this decision is that some services may be beyond the capabilities of some school districts; the goal is reasonable and feasible accommodations.

In 1983 the amended Education for All Handicapped Children Act supported education and service programs to help youth transition from secondary education to postsecondary education or employment. The amended Rehabilitation Act of the same year underwrote model pilot projects to help youth with disabilities address problems transitioning from school to work; further amendments in 1986 expanded transition programs.

Technology was the focus of the 1988 Technology-Related Assistance for Individuals with Disabilities Act (Pub. L. No. 100-407), which helped states develop technology-related assistance programs for individuals with disabilities and their families. With this act, assistive technology devices and services were defined legislatively.

The year 1990 was a stellar one for legislation that addressed the needs of individuals with disabilities. The broad-ranging Americans with Disabilities Act of 1990 (Pub. L. No. 101-336) prohibited discrimination based on disability, or "a physical or mental impairment that substantially limits a major life activity." The act addressed discrimination issues of employment, public entities (e.g., schools, libraries) and public transportation, public accommodations, and telecommunications.

The 1990 amendments to the Education for All Handicapped Children Act, also known as the Individuals with Disabilities Education Act (IDEA), was groundbreaking legislation on the education of youth with disabilities. Under the act, schools are required to provide both assistive devices to help youth with disabilities function and special transition programs. The act also gave rise to a required individualized education program (IEP) for each student found eligible under the federal and state eligibility disability standards. Moreover, the act included the Bill of Rights for Persons with Disabilities. Autism was added as a separate disability category at this time, defined therein as a developmental disability, usually evident before age three, which significantly affects communication and social interaction, as well as educational performance.

The 1997 amendments to IDEA defined thirteen disabilities and extended the use of assistive technology to outside the school environment to a child's home or other setting. The updated legislation specified six core principles:

1. Free appropriate public education
2. Least restrictive environment
3. Appropriate evaluation
4. Individualized education program
5. Parent and student participation in decision making
6. Procedural safeguards

Youth between the ages of three and twenty-one receive services through part B of the act; part C provides services for those up to age two. In addition, schools have to provide assistive technology for students at no cost to parents if the IEP requires it.

The reauthorization of IDEA in 2004 stated that all children from preschool through age twenty-one must be provided a free appropriate public education that prepares them for further education, employment, and independent living. The 2004 regulations also encouraged the provision of early intervention services in natural environments, such as the home.

The 2001 No Child Left Behind Act (Pub. L. No. 107-110) mandated that all children should have fair, equal, and significant opportunities for high-quality education and to reach minimum proficiency on state and assessments. By this time, students with special needs were mainstreamed as much as possible, so teachers would need more training in determining appropriate assessments and interventions. According to the act, students labeled "disabled" may be placed in several possible environments, depending on their needs. Section 618 (a)(1) of the IDEA defined those environments as follows:

> **Regular classroom:** The student is in regular class or is removed to receive special education and related services less than 21 percent of the day.

Resource room: The student receives special education and related services outside the regular classroom more than 60 percent of the day.

Separate facilities: The student does not attend school with non-disabled students; he or she is educated in a separate day school, residential facility, or homebound or hospital setting.

Currently, about 96 percent of students with disabilities attend regular schools. They may have pullout sessions or receive basic education with adaptations. Special education teachers are being pushed into regular classrooms, as the main instructor, as a co-teacher, or as a supplemental teacher upon demand.

Technology-Related Legislation

As noted already, the first major legislation for incorporating technology to support youth was the Technology-Related Assistance Act of 1988 (Pub. L. No. 100-407).

Coming from the industry side, the Telecommunications Act of 1996 (Pub. L. No. 104-104) required manufacturers and service providers of telecommunications equipment to address the accessibility needs of people with disabilities. Some of the modifications included specialized keyboards and pointers, microphones, specialized mouse devices, closed captioning, interface modifications (e.g., screen enlargers, screen-reading systems, speech synthesizers, function keys), and computer display customizations (e.g., larger and slower cursors, contrast settings, font modification).

The Assistive Technology Act of 1998 (Pub. L. No. 105-394) provided additional funding to develop permanent and comprehensive statewide technology-related assistance programs. However, in 1990 and 1997 IDEA was the main impetus for schools to be responsible for providing assistive technology for students with disabilities, if so required as part of the student's IEP or other related services. Section 300.5 of the 2004 IDEA legislation defined assistive technology devices as follows: "Any item, piece of equipment, or product system, whether acquired commercially off the shelf, modified, or customized, that is used to increase, maintain, or improve the functional capabilities of a child with a disability. The term does not include a medical device that is surgically implanted, or the replacement of such device." Several functions were stipulated in incorporating assistive technologies:

- The child's needs and customary environment must be evaluated.
- Schools must select, acquire, customize, maintain, and replace assistive technology devices.
- Services with assistive technology devices must be coordinated with other existing educational and rehabilitation plan and programs.
- The child and other service providers (including families) need to be trained in using the assistive technology devices.

Different federal agencies monitor these acts, and the provisions and requirements of each act differ. The following table provides some guidance on the rights and responsibilities for youth with special needs, including those with autism.

Legal Action Focused on ASDs

As mentioned earlier, the 1990 IDEA (Pub. L. No. 101-476) designated autism as a separate disability category. In that same year, *Johnson v. Independent School District of Bixby* (921 F.2d 1022 (1990)) decided that several factors should be considered in determining the need for an extended academic year for students with autism: degree of impairment, ability of the child to interact, rate of the child's progress, and the service provider professional's prediction of the rate of the child's progress.

Since 2000 several court cases have addressed inventions for students with ASDs. For example, in the 2007 California court case *E. N. v. Byron Union School District* (Case No. C 06-06052 CRB), the judge decided that the student could benefit from general classroom education and did not need to be placed in a special school. In 2002, the judge determined that a student with Asperger's syndrome, in *West Des Moines Community School District v. Heartland Area Education Agency* (Iowa 190 Fed. Appx. 512), was entitled to special education services even though he was performing well academically. In a similar case that year, in the same school district, another student with Asperger's

Table 3.1. **COMPARISON OF SPECIAL NEEDS LEGISLATION**

FACTOR	ADA	SECTION 504	IDEA
Monitoring agency	Department of Justice	Office for Civil Rights	U.S. Department of Education: Office of Special Education
Eligibility	All individuals with defined disabilities	All individuals with defined disabilities	All youth ages 3–21 with a designated disability who need special education
Compliance	All businesses, government agencies, and public accommodations	All entities who receive federal funds	All public schools in states that participate in IDEA
Basic requirement	Do not discriminate against anyone on the basis of disability	Do not discriminate against anyone on the basis of disability	Provide eligible students with free appropriate public education
Specific requirements	Assessment, accommodation plan, least restrictive environment	Assessment, accommodation plan, least restrictive environment	Assessment, IEP, least restrictive environment
Assessment	Preplacement assessment before determining 504 eligibility; required before any placement change	Preplacement assessment before determining 504 eligibility; required before any placement change	Comprehensive assessment before determining eligibility and IEP development; required every 3 years if needed

syndrome lacked social skills, but the IEP addressed only academic skills; the school needed to include both gifted education and social skills training in the IEP.

Singling out autism, the Combating Autism Act of 2006 (Pub. L. No. 109-416) authorized funding to deal with autism spectrum disorders and related disorders (e.g., childhood disintegrative disorder, pervasive developmental disorder not otherwise specified) through research, screening, education, early interventions, and referrals. One of the major provisions of the act is the commitment to establish statewide screening systems to ensure that all children are screened for autism by age two. Before this act, the usual age for providing screening services for ASDs was age three, which in effect delayed possible early treatments. In 2011 the act was reauthorized to continue funding for three additional years. Recognizing the need for more qualified teachers to instruct students with ASDs, some states are developing special authorizations, or licensures, to ensure competent instruction. A case in point is California, which approved a new autism authorization for teachers in 2009. A report by the Commission on Teacher Credentialing's special education workgroup noted an 88 percent increase over five years in students requiring services for ASDs. Approved programs provide twelve semester units of coursework beyond teachers' original special education credential. Content matter includes characteristics of ASDs, teaching, learning and behavior strategies for students with ASDs, and collaboration with other service providers (e.g., librarians) and families.

IEPs and IFSPs

Individualized education programs (IEPs) are a cornerstone for the provision of school services to students with special needs; the amended 1990 IDEA included autism under its scope, requiring IEPs for students with ASDs. Individualized family support plans (IFSPs) started in 1986 for infants and toddlers. In both cases, a team determines the child's outcomes on the basis of his or her strengths and needs, available resources, emerging priorities, and family concerns. The IEP team consists of school personnel, parents, and other service providers. Team members might also include paraprofessional special educators, autism specialists, discipline-specific assessment experts (e.g., speech-language pathologists), assistive technology specialists, behavioral experts, and school psychologists. Librarians rarely serve on the team, but they can provide valuable input, especially if a child uses the library frequently or communicates with library staff regularly (e.g., teenagers with deep subject interest that the library supports).

The process of writing an IEP includes listing measurable annual goals, determining curriculum objectives (which can include behavioral and social skills as well as academic skills), and means to evaluate progress. Parents need to be informed of their child's process at least every nine weeks. The IEP also must explain the extent to which the child will or will not participate with children without disabilities in regular classes and activities so that the least restrictive environment can be determined. Human and material resources (e.g., specialist staff, assistive technology) to support efforts are also included in the IEP; for instance, counties may have trained software specialists who work with children with disabilities. These services might not be mentioned unless parents and other caregivers specifically ask for them, so background research is important, and librarians can help locate such information. The U.S. Department of Education provides guidance for the individualized education program (www2.ed.gov/parents/needs/speced/iepguide/index.html#form).

Moreover, IFSPs also determine child outcomes, taking into consideration the family's resources, priorities, and concerns. Outcomes should include progress in preliteracy and language skills. Children between three and five years old may have either an IEP or an IFSP, depending on their individual needs. Part 303.18 of the 2004 IDEA also stipulates that early interventions should be provided in natural environments; that is, "sections that are natural or normal for the child's age peers who have no disabilities." The Iowa Department of Education provides several IFSP forms (as well as IEP forms) at http://educateiowa.gov/index.php?option=com_content&task=view&id=633.

Librarians and the Law

Libraries tend to operate under the auspices of some legal entity that is responsible for complying with laws related to services for individuals with disabilities. Addressing the needs of individuals with ASDs usually does not entail many modifications of facilities or even resources, although proactive measures can certainly facilitate the child's experience. The emphasis is usually placed on providing appropriate resources that meet the needs and interests of the child, and interacting with them appropriately. For library programs to be compliant is probably not too difficult; they are usually of minor importance in legal terms, but they can significantly help youth with ASDs and their families.

Especially as the ratio of children with ASDs increases relative to the total school-age population, librarians can expect to see these children in the library. In the public library, children with ASDs are likely to come with their family for an independent visit or as part of a story hour or other program, although day-care facilities might also bring a class with such children to the library. At school, youth with ASDs usually come to the library as part of a class, although flexible scheduling might enable them to come individually as well as outside class time. Nevertheless, few librarians see IEPs or IFSPs, or even know which children have them (or section 504 accommodations). As a result, the librarian might have unrealistic expectations of the child or not provide appropriate services. Short of a sign that reads "I am IEP/IFSP-friendly," librarians usually have to proactively seek information about library users with ASDs. This task is usually easier to accomplish in school settings, where the librarian can schedule a time to meet with the special education coordinator and get to understand how to garner information that can help support these students. At the very least, librarians should try to see what an IEP and IFSP look like. Public librarians who service a day-care program regularly can inquire about those children with special needs. More proactively, librarians can partner with service providers and experts to offer workshops on ASDs in community informational sessions. In any case, showing an honest interest in youth with special needs is a welcome sign for those who work with these children and is a first step in helping these youth develop their full potential.

FACILITIES

Libraries are open to all, no matter ethnicity, age, background, experience, or expectations. Both in public and in school libraries, youth with ASDs are likely to encounter people who are different from them. Libraries tend to be inclusive and to permit a wide range of behaviors and interactions, depending on users' needs. Even so, libraries should look for ways to expand their efforts to provide an inclusive atmosphere that encompasses universal design in its planning.

Libraries as learning spaces need to foster student engagement and active learning. Common spaces provide opportunities for youth with ASDs to practice social skills, but these youth also need more enclosed spaces and private areas to which they can retreat when overwhelmed or needing to work without distraction. Therefore, libraries need to offer differentiated space and flexible furniture to facilitate easy rearrangement to fit varying activities. Even lighting should vary, from natural ambient light to focused study lights; indirect lighting is the most conducive to reading, and fluorescent lighting should be avoided. Furthermore, lighting (and monitors) should be flicker-free.

In today's libraries technology plays a key role, in terms of both providing resources and integrating personal technology devices. Librarians should also acknowledge the importance of cyberspace and try to meld the virtual world with the physical one. Trends in incorporating technology into learning spaces include ubiquitous wikis, subject-specific and function-specific technology, and technology for collaboration. It should be noted that, although technology can enrich the educational experience, it can also distract from learning. Not only is it tempting to surf the Internet during instruction, but youth with ASDs may be intrigued by some minor aspect of a piece of technology, such as the feel of the keyboard, and ignore the task at hand. In that respect, paired learning can foster on-task participation, and it reinforces the concept of the student as a contributor to the knowledge base. Open spaces, with a couple of bordered areas, can be allocated for use of laptops and other mobile devices.

When applying universal design to learning spaces, librarians should conceptualize the facility as a product to develop rather than a space to be changed. The product is based on the institution's values about libraries and learning. Bennett (2007) presented six factors to consider when designing learning spaces, which can apply to libraries and incorporate the needs of youth with ASDs:

1. What aspects of learning require this physical space rather than a virtual one? Youth with ASDs need opportunities to gain a sense of their bodies in space, and neutral spaces in which to navigate and socialize.
2. How does this space help individuals study longer and more productively? How comfortable is the seating? Are low-contrast corners available (e.g., neutral colors, no reflection, no bright lights)? Do some chairs have well-defined edges to help one define the seating space? If children sit on the floor, are smooth

rubber squares available to define space? Is alternative seating such as a beanbag or rocking chair available to ensure sensory need of pressure or motion? Are carrels or other private spaces available? Is the noise level acceptable, or can the library have differentiated quiet zones? Can headphones be provided? Can doors be closed to shut out noise?

3. Where on the spectrum from isolation to large-group work should this space be designed? Is variable seating provided? Can tables be combined to provide different levels of interaction (e.g., pairs, corner interaction)? Can movable partitions or writing surfaces cut up open space?

4. What does this space communicate about the nature and management of knowledge? Is inquiry and co-constructed knowledge facilitated through joint study areas? Can the area support individual reading?

5. Should this space facilitate adult-youth interaction outside of class time? Are semiprivate areas available for youth to meet and work with service providers without distraction or other people listening? Glass-enclosed conference spaces can ensure privacy while maintaining supervision.

6. How might this space enrich educational experiences? What display space is available? What technologies can be used independently or in groups, such as public computer or television monitors? Are whiteboards and Smart boards available? The space needs to be both stimulating and calming.

If possible, the librarian can walk with the youth and a service provider to scout out comfortable areas for future use. That kind of facility "rehearsal" can lower anxiety for youth who will use the facility regularly. This kind of activity is particularly useful before the fall when a child enters a new school so that he or she can count on some sense of predictability. If a walk-around is not possible, providing a video or pictures of the library can also ease the transition to a new space. The one drawback to identifying a special spot is that the child may consider it his or her own permanent place and get frustrated if someone else tries to use it. If the other child does not mind moving, then that favored spot can be reclaimed. However, over time youth with ASDs need to learn to share and take turns. As a way to lower anxiety, a timer can be used to indicate how long another person will use the space, to provide some predictable time frame and end to the change.

RESOURCES

As noted before, libraries offer a unique opportunity to choose from a rich variety of resources: in terms of content matter, perspective, readability, and format. Furthermore, libraries provide access to resources worldwide via telecommunications. Public libraries are the de facto all-inclusive environment for information and ideas because they serve the entire public community, from toddler to tottering. School libraries serve their school community and should provide materials not only to students but also to staff and families. In all of these library settings, collections are carefully chosen, and it is this process that can draw on the universal design principle of multiple means of representation.

For all resources, format is critical, as individuals have varying degrees of sensitivities. Therefore, print materials need to have sturdy pages and bindings. Pages should be easy to turn. The size should be manageable: not too heavy and not too large or small. For toddlers, libraries should provide both well-constructed board books and fabric ones. Materials that are ripped or dirty should be repaired or withdrawn. As much as possible, fonts should be easy to read, with high contrast to the page background. Ideally, materials should include both textual and visual features to facilitate dual coding (i.e., comprehension from text that explains visuals, and vice versa). Textural and aural features are also desirable. Informational books should have visual cues for comprehension: headings, font options for emphasis (e.g., boldface, italic), outlines, captioned images, tables, and checklists.

In considering electronic reference resources, additional physical criteria should be considered:

> **Navigation:** How easily can the user find the information needed? What navigation tools are available? Is searching—and meta-searching—intuitive and universally accessible? To what depth can the user search for information (e.g., chapter, topic, paragraph, chart)? How easily can users keep track of their search

history and be able to locate themselves relative to a website? Is a "help" function readily available? To what extent do users have to "bend" to technical formats as opposed to the technology being crafted to meet user needs? Can all input be done via keyboard?

Readability: Are text and images easy to view? Are additional plugins necessary? Is content accessible for individuals with special needs? Can viewing options be changed? Can individuals with special needs access information (i.e., in compliance with the Americans with Disabilities Act)?

Representation: Is knowledge represented in several formats? Are images captioned? Is sound transcribed? Is a glossary or dictionary available conveniently (e.g., hyperlinked)?

Many resources come available in print and digital form. In addition, the Digital Accessible Information System (www.daisy.org) established open standards with the intent that "all published information, at time of release to the general population, be available in an accessible, highly functional, feature rich format and at no greater cost, to persons with print disabilities." The consortium also provides free tools to help librarians and publishers produce and convert resources for inclusive use.

INTERACTION

The best collection and the nicest facilities cannot overcome negative and dysfunctional library staff. If the library atmosphere is toxic, few youth will willingly take advantage of the library and its potential riches. Furthermore, one bad interaction tends to outweigh ten positive ones. It is hard to know how to deal effectively with a wide range of personalities, but some universal design factors can lay the groundwork for successful interaction for all types of people, which will help the social and communication skills of youth with ASDs.

As hinted at already, the overall climate of the library needs to reflect high values and respect for inclusivity and diversity. The library may be a safe haven for youth with ASD: an orderly, neutral place where they can self-determine personal actions to a large degree and not be bothered by other people. This expectation needs to be made explicit—and actively modeled—to youth and their service providers.

As noted elsewhere in this book, the single greatest contribution that librarians can make is to get to know youth on an individual and personal level. Greeting them by name as they enter the library, communicating with them in low-stress times, and listening to them help create a trusting bond that provides a solid base for effective service. The Young Adult Library Services Association (2010) has stated that librarians should exhibit certain behaviors toward all youth:

- Respect, value, and listen to each person.
- Form appropriate professional relationships and partnerships with youth.
- Identify and meet the unique needs and interests of youth.
- Communicate high expectations in behavior, ability, and attitudes.
- Be familiar with youth developmental needs and help build their assets so that they can become healthy, successful adults.
- Promote and reinforce positive citizenship and diversity.
- Engage their natural curiosity and creativity.
- Develop and supervise youth participation.
- Build a sense of family and community.

Likewise, the Reference and User Services Association (2004) has developed guidelines for behavioral performance that reflect universal design principles for interaction:

Approachability: Be ready to help and focus attention on the user's needs, and express welcoming body language.

Interest: Exhibit a high degree of interest, signal understanding, and try to provide the most effective help.

Listening and inquiring: Communicate in a receptive and encouraging manner, use an appropriate tone of voice, demonstrate understanding of the user's needs, and avoid value judgments.

Searching: Encourage the user to contribute ideas, and facilitate self-directed learning.

Follow-up: Determine the degree of user satisfaction, and encourage the user to return as needed.

As a center for positive learning and interaction, the library should support and facilitate effective interactions between youth and across generations. Because communication methods vary by person, librarians should openly accept and support different modes, be it pointing or drawing or using assistive technology. In that respect, librarians serve as youth advocates, and to maintain civility, they may need to serve as mediators between youth with ASDs and other people. If unusual or inappropriate behavior occurs, the librarian should try to redirect the behavior or ask another adult to help the child act more productively. More proactively, the library should arrange the library's furniture to provide unobtrusive supervision. Setting and explaining a short list of well-defined, enforceable, and fair rules helps all youth know how to behave appropriately. Likewise, librarians can anticipate possible behavior problems and have a plan to preemptively deal with them.

The following practices help manage groups and enable youth with ASDs to participate more comfortably:

- Provide a consistent, predictable routine for library use and instruction.
- Keep instructions clear and simple, and provide them in multiple formats (e.g., oral, written, visual).
- Use singing and rhythm games to get all children's attention; music can communicate rich content as well.
- Visual aids, too, assist many children in learning—picture dictionaries provide valuable cues for meaning, and video clips can show positive behaviors in concrete detail.
- Provide a visual schedule to help all youth know the sequence of activities.
- When shifting activities, signal this to youth a couple of minutes ahead to help them prepare for the transition.
- Repeatedly check for understanding by questioning, listening, and observing; this can help librarians adjust their behaviors and content material to ensure that all youth are successful.
- Take into account the affective aspects of interactions so that youth remain positive and motivated.
- Enthusiasm has its good and bad points; it can be infectious, boosting the spirits of the group, but it can also overwhelm

youth with ASDs, especially if they express their boisterousness noisily. Single-finger clapping is a fun and novel way to show positive feelings quietly. To help youth with ASDs practice body awareness and dexterity, a sequential clap in which pinkies match, then ring fingers, all the way to the thumb, can be used.

These practices help all youth interact appropriately. More specific management issues for youth with ASDs are detailed in chapter 8.

LEARNING ACTIVITIES

As librarians help youth gain intellectual access to information, they try to connect with all users. Because librarians tend to have short interactions with youth, even when instructing, they need to plan learning activities that all students can participate in, using instructional techniques that enable all students to comprehend and apply the ideas embedded in the activity. Universal design for learning is a set of principles that give all individuals equitable opportunities to learn.

The Higher Education Opportunity Act of 2008 (Pub. L. No. 110-315) defined the more specific universal design for learning as a scientifically valid framework for guiding educational practice, stating that it

(A) Provides flexibility in the ways information is presented, in the ways students respond or demonstrate knowledge and skills, and in the ways students are engaged; and

(B) Reduces barriers in instruction, provides appropriate accommodations, supports, and challenges, and maintains high achievement expectations for all students, including students with disabilities and students who are limited English proficient.

The premise is that one size does not fit all, and individual variability is the norm. By planning a curriculum and instruction with built-in flexibility from the start, librarians spend less time making accommodations or changes after the fact. Universal design for learning also enables librarians to start with youth where they are rather than where they "should" be. This attitude aligns well with current library practices and optimizes learning participation by youth with ASDs.

Learning activities consist of two main aspects: accessing and processing information, and acting on or expressing it. As librarians plan activities that engage all youth, they have to recognize the variety of motivations and learning processes. They also need to realize that acting on information requires organization, planning, and practice. This book focuses on the diversity of youth with ASDs, and that diversity is even more pronounced when considering culture, prior experience, and background knowledge.

Starting with curriculum, librarians and their collaborators determine the learning expectations or goals that specify the knowledge, skills, and dispositions that the learner should demonstrate. Librarians then help learners meet those goals through methods of instruction and other procedures, which need to be monitored throughout the process to make needed adjustments. The resources used to meet those goals have already been discussed in terms of universal design. To determine whether the learner has met a goal, assessment is needed that is comprehensive enough and clear enough to guide instruction for all learners.

Specific universal design guidelines provide best practices throughout the process of planning learning activities (Center for Applied Special Technology 2011):

- Gain attention and interest in several ways: optimize individual choice and autonomy, build on natural interests, optimize relevance and value, invite personal response, make activities authentic, and foster imagination and problem solving.
- Minimize obstacles and distractions: provide a safe and supportive atmosphere, vary the level of novelty and risk, vary the level of sensory stimulation, and vary social demands.
- Provide options for sustaining effort: keep goals central, vary resources and demands to optimize challenge, vary the amount of independence, facilitate collaboration, group people flexibly, provide timely and specific feedback and opportunities to make personal adjustments accordingly, help learners know what motivates and frustrates them, and teach personal coping skills.

- Customize how information is displayed: through enlargement, color adjustment, cropping, volume control, speed of movement, and so on. This practice is easier with digital resources.
- Offer alternatives for auditory information: through captioning, visual equivalents, or tactile equivalents.
- Offer alternatives for visual information: through text, oral description, or tactile objects.
- Offer options for language: through glossaries and other explanations, visual cues, graphical representations, highlighting, translation tools, and text-to-speech tools.
- Offer options for comprehension: by supplying background knowledge; highlighting main points and patterns, examples and nonexamples, and graphic organizers; and breaking down processes or concepts into smaller steps.
- Offer options for physical action: through different ways to input information, assistive technologies, and alternative movements and use of the body.
- Use multiple media to communicate: through text, speech, drawing, video, manipulatives, and social media.
- Use multiple tools to compose and construct: spell-checkers, text-to-speech technology, calculators, concept mapping, and web applications.
- Offer options for metacognition and self-regulation: models, checklists, graphic organizers, templates, rubrics, and process portfolios.

The Center for Applied Special Technology has an online universal-design-for-learning lesson builder that provides librarians and other educators with models and tools to create inclusive learning activities (http://lessonbuilder.cast.org).

CONCLUDING THOUGHTS

In short, librarians need to balance the universal with the particular. To address a diverse group of youth, librarians need to establish a common goal and some common values. They need to provide choices for individuals to personalize their experiences and common activities that all youth can enjoy. At the very least, librarians should find out which youth have special needs, and then gain basic knowledge about ways to create a suitable library environment for them that works for all users. Ideally, school librarians should consult children's IEPs to find out which strategies are effective and to determine the extent to which those strategies can be incorporated into the overall library experience so that children with ASDs can take advantage of the library alongside the rest of their peers.

REFERENCES

Bennett, S. "First Questions for Designing Higher Education Learning Spaces." *Journal of Academic Leadership* 33 (2007): 14–26.

Center for Applied Special Technology. *Universal Design for Learning Guidelines Version 2.0.* Wakefield, MA: Center for Applied Special Technology, 2011.

Center for Universal Design. *The Principles of Universal Design.* Raleigh: North Carolina State University, 1997.

Hernon, P., and P. Calvert, eds. *Improving the Quality of Library Services for Students with Disabilities.* Westport, CT: Libraries Unlimited, 2006.

Reference and User Services Association. *Guidelines for Behavioral Performance of Reference and Information Service Providers.* Chicago: American Library Association, 2004.

Tomlinson, C. *The Differentiated Classroom.* Alexandria, VA: Association of Supervision and Curriculum Development, 1999.

Young Adult Library Services Association. *YALSA's Competencies for Librarians Serving Youth: Young Adults Deserve the Best.* Chicago: American Library Association, 2010.

CHAPTER 4

Resources

S OME CORE ASPECTS OF LIBRARIES INCLUDE THE COLLECTION, ORGA-
nization, and access to resources. Libraries' content
needs to build on individual interests. Because youth
with ASDs engage in different ways with content, identifying and using information in a variety of formats is
imperative; visual information is especially helpful. In
addition, resources that build on sensory experiences
can lead to more effective engagement for youth with
ASDs. Technology provides potentially effective resources and communication channels. As librarians choose resources, they should consider the age and development of youth with ASDs to optimize their
engagement and learning. In optimizing technology, librarians need to
consider the critical features of technology, including their psychological impact, that are motivators for student engagement.

Assistive technology, which includes any device that can assist a
person in adapting to a given skill, can help level the learning field of
students with ASDs. This chapter deals with a variety of resources, the
uses of which are detailed in chapters 5 and 6.

THE SENSES AND AUTISM SPECTRUM DISORDERS

A common characteristic of ASDs is that they affect the senses. In some cases, a person is hypersensitive to sensory input; in other cases, even a lot of sensory input doesn't get a response; and in still other cases, the person seeks out sensation. These variations in sensory processing, which are attributable to the limbic and cerebellar systems of the brain, affect emotional functioning, such that people with ASDs can feel overwhelmed or act out. As mentioned in other chapters, individuals with ASDs have a difficult time integrating the sensory processes of arousal, attention to environment, affect, engagement, and motor output. For that reason, items such as balls or specially designed chairs help keep a person stimulated, and weighted vests provide a deep-pressure calming effect. Librarians can keep a few of such items on hand, but they should talk with parents and other service providers before using them.

Print resources vary surprisingly in how they stimulate the senses, and they can accommodate differences in sensory experiences:

> **Tactile:** extured book surfaces (e.g., sandpaper, fabric, feathers, cellophane), as in *Pat the Bunny*, by Dorothy Kunhardt (Golden Books, 1970)
> **Auditory:** cards with sound clips, LeapFrog "tag" books, audiobooks
> **Olfactory:** books with a scent, such as scratch-and-sniff books
> **Movement:** use of technology (e.g., keyboarding, touch screens)

There are several ways to make print items more accessible to children with ASDs:

> **Stabilize:** Attach books or materials to a steady surface. Choose books with spiral or other lay-flat bindings.
> **Enlarge:** Enlarge texts and pictures to make them easier to see. Provide books with thicker pages for easier turning. Laminates can be added to thicken pages.
> **Add parts:** Add clips to the edges of pages for easier turning.
> **Simplify:** Offer a version of the book with less text.

Make more familiar and/or concrete: Choose books that have photographs instead of illustrations.

Add cues: Attach multisensory materials to books.

Add texture: Use flannelboards, or add fuzzy fur for a bear story or cotton balls for a story about clouds, for example.

Add realia: Provide objects that fit with a story, such as a stuffed toy or musical instrument.

How youth with ASDs process sensory information also helps librarians determine which format of a relevant resource to use. For instance, if a child has trouble with sound, then visual sources such as photographs and books are better choices than audiobooks. For some youth with ASDs, still images are easier to comprehend than moving pictures, so librarians should avoid videos in favor of photographs. The size of the resource also should be considered; a book, for example, should be easy for the child to grasp, and so a miniature book or an oversized one might be hard to handle. The best approach is to ask service providers about the child's preferences. In addition, providing the child with a choice between two options gives the child a sense of control and provides an opportunity for him or her to make a decision.

THE ROLE OF TECHNOLOGY

Technology can help youth with ASDs significantly because it can be highly structured with discrete stimuli or activities, it involves kinesthetics, it accepts nonverbal responses, it usually does not require high social skills, it can be used predictably and repetitively, and it facilitates creative expression. Computer technology also extends children's attention span. Some sample technology-based techniques that support the needs of youth with ASDs are the following:

- Use documents that are literal and repetitive or rhythmic and that include photos rather than drawings.
- Use a variety of formats: audiocassettes, software, toys, manipulatives.
- Take advantage of picture dictionaries and atlases.

- Enlarge texts and pictures to make them easier to see.
- Use visual rather than auditory stimulation.
- Incorporate Kid Pix and drawing software programs; students are likely to enjoy and focus on a particular thing or character.
- Use videotapes of a book together with the print copy.
- Show video clips that demonstrate positive behaviors in very concrete detail.
- Use software (e.g., Reader Rabbit, Math Blaster, BrainPro) and web tutorials to teach skills.

These strategies are examples of universal design, which helps not only students with autism but all students. In that respect, they can be used in mainstreamed classes so that youth with ASDs are not singled out and instead can experience learning with a diversity of youth and gain social skills at the same time that they gain academically.

Assistive Technology

According to the Individuals with Disabilities Education Act (Pub. L. No. 101-476), assistive technology is any item, piece of equipment, or product system that is used to increase, maintain, or improve the functional capabilities of a child with a disability. As such, assistive technology can be as simple as a clipboard or pencil grip or as sophisticated as a voice-operated computer. It should be noted that assistive technology is a bypass strategy, not a remediation technique. Nevertheless, the effective use of assistive technology can result in greater independence and self-confidence, enhanced self-esteem, more creative and analytic thinking, and academic success.

Several laws mandate the provision of assistive technology, especially as part of IEPs. Furthermore, schools cannot presumptively deny assistive technology, such as because of cost; the technology must be provided if required to receive free appropriate education as a basic floor of opportunity. The laws do not require that the best assistive technology be provided, just appropriate assistive technology: an expensive solution does not need to be acquired if a less costly and more easily available one can do the job adequately. In any case, assistive technology should be part of library resources and services, at least in partnership with other service providers.

Technology Accessibility Standards

A main tenet of libraries is free and equitable access to desired library resources. Section 508 of the Rehabilitation Act requires federal entities to make reasonable efforts to provide information that is universally accessible. If information cannot meet that standard, then the entity has to provide an alternative way to access the information equivalently. The U.S. Patent and Trademark Office provides an electronic and information technology procurement checklist, technical standards, and reference guides to help evaluate a product's accessibility (www.uspto .gov/web/offices/cio/s508/index.html). The Association of Specialized and Cooperative Library Agencies provides several tip sheets for librarians on making sure that all resources are accessible (www.ala.org/ala/ mgrps/divs/ascla/asclaprotools/accessibilitytipsheets/index.cfm).

For example, software applications need to address the following factors:

- Enable users to input completely using a keyboard (i.e., without a mouse); Microsoft Windows has a set of systemwide shortcut keys to display menus, use windows, navigate, and so on.
- Provide output textually (i.e., without images, sounds, and so on).
- Accept accessibility features, such as a magnifier or narrator.
- Provide easy-to-find on-screen indication of current focus (e.g., cursor), which is linked to assistive technology.
- Make all visual information available to assistive technology, such as captioned images.
- Use an image consistently throughout the product, and ensure that its meaning is consistent (e.g., picture of a printer).
- Make all textual information available to assistive technology (e.g., font attributes).
- Conform to users' operating system display settings; a product's own color and contrast settings must comply with standard 1194.21j from section 508 of the Rehabilitation Act of 1973 (Pub. L. No. 93-112).
- If animation is used, users must be able to select a nonanimated model to display information.
- Do not use color coding as the sole way to convey information or distinctions.

- Provide a variety of color selections and contrast levels when an application allows users to change those settings.
- Avoid using flashing and blinking elements.
- Make all electronic forms accessible to assistive technology.

Similarly, web pages need to follow these guidelines. They also need to ensure the following:

- Documents are readable without requiring an associated style sheet.
- Row and column headers are provided in data tables.
- Frames are titled to facilitate identification and navigation.
- Scripting language and plug-ins are available to assistive technology.
- An alert and extra time are provided when a timed response is required.
- Accessibility and compatibility features are described in a universally acceptable manner.

Librarians can make adjustments to existing computer systems to accommodate the needs of youth with ASDs, and then label that system diversity-friendly. The library might provide a bank or pod of such modified systems, for which certain individuals get first priority. Some of the simple adjustments include the following:

- providing a larger monitor
- providing a track ball, joystick, or touch pad
- providing a modified keyboard (e.g., smaller or larger keys, textured keys, colored keys, alphabetically sequenced keys, one-handed keyboard)
- providing an input microphone
- providing headphones
- providing a scanner
- changing screen and input-output settings (accessed under "ease of use" in Windows 7, and under "system preferences" in the Apple operating system)
- modifying browser settings

Matching Technology with the Individual

The adage mentioned earlier—"If you've met one person with autism, you've met one person with autism"—also applies to the use of technology. Certainly, in the area of ASDs, one size does not fit all, so careful diagnosis is needed to find the optimum technology for each individual.

The most obvious place to start when trying to find the best technology match is the individual: What are his or her needs, capabilities, and preferences? What motivates the individual? What is he or she ready for? What are his or her expectations? What moods does he or she display, and under what conditions? How did he or she use prior support? What is his or her lifestyle? No matter how appropriate the technology, if a person doesn't like the product or feels embarrassed using it, the technology will not be effective. Therefore, the affective side of technology must be considered throughout the process. Here are some examples of ways that technology can be used to support processing challenges associated with ASDs:

Visual Processing Approaches
- graphic organizers
- adjustable lighting and colors
- text-to-speech function on computer
- scanner
- videotaped material

Auditory Processing Approaches
- peer note taker
- tape recorder (requires motivation)
- amplification device

Organizational Processing Approaches
- sticky notes or index cards
- assignment books
- color-coded binder
- mobile equipment such as smart phones
- Inspiration-brand software (i.e., concept-mapping application)

Next, the librarian should analyze the environment in which the person will use the technology. What are the physical characteristics, such as space and furniture? What is the economic situation? What legislative mandates apply? What cultural norms or expectations affect the environment? What attitudes must be considered, such as people's perceptions of those with different capabilities or their perceptions of technology? At this stage, librarians should recognize and address individuals' feelings, especially any fears they may have about being teased or harassed or about feeling isolated from their peers when using the technology.

At this point, librarians can begin to choose a technology. What technology is available, and how much does it cost (both initially and in terms of maintenance)? What are its characteristics? How does it perform? What is its appearance? Its size and weight? How comfortable is it ergonomically? How easy is it to use? What training is required to use it effectively?

Several online tools help people find appropriate assistive technologies. Commercial diagnostic tools can be purchased to help with the process, but there are several good, free tools available to the service provider team, as well as to the youth and his or her family:

> **Ability Hub** (www.abilityhub.com) directs people to adaptive equipment and alternative methods available for accessing computers.
>
> The federal **General Services Administration** has an online wizard to help choose accessible products and services (https://app .buyaccessible.gov/baw/).
>
> **Microsoft's Assistive Technology Decision Tree** (http://download .microsoft.com/download/7/e/b/7ebfb5a1-69af-4e2a-aba7-7f1 1e2d66fed/atdecisiontree.pdf) helps identify the appropriate assistive technology according to users' needs.
>
> **Techmatrix** (www.techmatrix.org) is a searchable database for comparing technology products. For autism, it lists 178 products, 97 online resources, and 26 professional development resources; searches can be refined by content area, grade level, and learning support.

A good general rule is to start with simple solutions first, and then graduate to more complex assistive technologies as needed. Here are some assistive technology solutions listed in order of complexity and cost:

Simple Support Strategies
- dry-erase boards
- clipboards
- three-ring binders
- manila file folders
- photo albums
- laminated Picture Exchange Communication System cards and photographs
- highlighting tape

Middle-Level Support Strategies
- battery-operated devices or simple electronic devices
- tape recorders
- Big Mack (large-button) recorder
- Language Master software
- overhead projectors
- timers
- calculators

High-End Support Strategies
- touch screens
- communication boards with symbols (e.g., Boardmaker, IntelliKeys)
- voice-output devices
- cameras (still and video)

Librarians can be instrumental in choosing technologies, and they can point to diagnosis tools and research vendors. In some cases, the library may own a relevant technology, such as a cassette player, which can be circulated. Other technologies, such as specialized keyboards, need to be customized.

Age and Developmental Issues

Both the age and the development of each child needs to be considered when choosing and providing resources. Particularly because development is likely to be different in the areas of cognition, communication, and social interaction, practices need to be individualized.

Regardless of the disability, age makes a big difference, if for no other reason than physical size and capability. Can the child reach the resource and handle it? Is the child strong enough to carry it? In most cases, the child lives in a social environment and experiences people around him or her. Most preteens and teens with ASDs have some self-awareness that they are different from others, and they can feel self-conscious about their disorder. Therefore, the resources that they use should not isolate them further; for that reason, mainstream technologies such as iPads can be an effective solution. Likewise, teens who have difficulty reading usually do not want to be seen with children's books, so high-interest, low-readability titles and visually rich resources are usually more acceptable to them.

Many of the developmental aspects of youth with ASDs are not obvious to the eye, so librarians need to work closely with service providers to identify developmentally appropriate resources. For example, observing how children play is a good way to choose resources that fit their developmental stage (Wolfberg 2003):

- At the manipulative-sensory stage, children explore objects but do not use them conventionally. Rhythm instruments and textured objects are appropriate.
- At the function stage, children respond to an object's features and can relate two or more objects. They might enjoy train sets, stacking blocks, and simple puzzles.
- At the symbolic-pretend stage, children can act with representational intent. Tool kits, cooking sets, dolls, and play phones are all appropriate.

Play also has a social dimension, which needs to be considered when choosing an appropriate resource:

- At the isolate stage, children play alone, so the resource needs to be easy enough for one person to operate.
- At the parallel-proximity stage, children play independently alongside peers and may imitate their peers, so having several copies or variations of the same item, such as animal figures or vehicles, is a good idea.
- At the stage of common focus, joint attention and joint action or reciprocal social exchange occurs. They can share blocks, art supplies, and big books.
- At the common-goal stage, children carry out a common agenda and help one another. Simulated play environments, such as a bookstore or dress-up corner, work well.

Communication is another developmentally defined aspect that needs to be considered when choosing resources:

- At the nonverbal stage, children might need tangible object systems: three-dimensional objects that are similar to or part of the items they represent (e.g., an airplane model). Children at the symbolic stage can use pictures or photos, such as the Picture Exchange Communication System.
- Children with significant articulation problems can use voice-output communication aids.
- At the context-dependent stage, youth can use text-to-speech apps on handheld devices. Token systems, which reward appropriate communication skills, can even be self-managed using applications.
- As youth become more independent in their communication, they can use predictive word software to strengthen their language skills.

TECHNOLOGY RESOURCES FOR YOUTH WITH ASDs

Librarians are in the business of resources, providing them as needed by their constituents. There is an enormous range of technologies available, which helps librarians meet the various needs of youth with ASDs and their service providers.

Mainstream Technologies

In considering the unique aspects of each youth with an ASD, the appropriate technology may well be a mainstream device and not necessarily a specialized assistive technology. In addition, several technologies work well with most youth. Universal design enables librarians to design instruction and learning activities that motivate and engage all learners.

INTERACTIVE BOARDS

Interactive boards facilitate interaction as students touch the screen and use board icons and templates to communicate. Interactive boards are a motivating way to help students learn how to take turns, interact reciprocally, and follow several-step directions. Some programs that work well with interactive boards include the following:

> **CBeebies** (www.bbc.co.uk/cbeebies), an interactive website with games, songs, and art activities
>
> **Reading Is Fundamental** (www.rif.org), which provides free reading resources
>
> **Starfall** (http://kids.lovetoknow.com/wiki/Starfall_Games_for_Kids), which offers reading activities and games

OPTICAL DISKS

Commercial and locally made educational CDs and DVDs can provide unobtrusive instruction for youth with ASDs. The library can maintain a box of portable CD and DVD players with headphones for use in the library. For example, CDs or DVDs might include a short rap on an academic subject, which works well for youth with ASDs who communicate primarily through echolalic response. The beat of a short, rhyming rap can be ascertained in a short period of time and played repeatedly all day if need be. Maureen Sykes created a rap CD to introduce vocabulary by connecting information through both hearing and touch. In sharing her experiences working with autistic youth, she provided a few examples:

- Thematic Dewey Decimal rap: "591 is snakes. 599 is mammals. 636 is inside animals . . . not to be confused with camels. The cobra is so deadly and the rattler is too. The garter snake is very friendly . . . and he won't kill you."
- Train rap: "Trains are called locomotives. They used to move with steam and coal. Now they run on other sources . . . of less expensive fuels. Trains are very shiny . . . and they go so fast. *Thomas the Tank Engine* is a book . . . in the Easy Reader aisle you just passed."
- Geography rap: "Capitals are the cities in states. I bet you know them too. Sacramento is the capital of California . . . and you live here too. Maps are the coolest things. They show us where people are. They tell us how many miles . . . where you can go so far."

GAMES

Many children like games, and youth with ASDs are no exception. Games can serve as a positive learning tool for youth with ASDs for several reasons (Myers 2008), including the following:

- fixed, equitable rules
- clear roles and expectations
- opportunities to explore identities
- meaningful goals
- structured interaction between players and between players and the game
- sense of control and personal investment
- internally consistent environments
- motivating opportunities for physical movement
- specific, timely feedback

In short, games offer a safe learning environment for developing cognitive, communication, and social skills. Chess, memory games, and many traditional card and board games can entertain while teaching youth with ASDs about taking turns, following directions, and other social skills.

Electronic games, or e-games (e.g., computer, video, or console games), have grown in popularity—almost all children have played them or know someone who has. Three-quarters of teens play video games at least weekly (Kahn, Middaugh, and Evans 2008). Today's technology offers not only high-quality visuals and sounds but also interactive features that enable youth with ASDs to experience social reciprocity without risking human rejection. Moreover, they can play the games repeatedly, and the computer remains supportive and patient.

Games in themselves do not guarantee academic success. However, serious games have education as their chief aim. For example, games like bingo and magic squares can help with number skills. The National Science Foundation supports science interest through games such as Power Up and River City Project. Simulation games such as Cool School (Cyber Oregon Online) and Darfur Is Dying (mtvU) help youth develop decision-making skills. Games such as Age of Mythology (Microsoft) and Revolution Games teach history. Online Scrabble and Pictionary can help develop vocabulary. Wii games are especially good for teaching motor skills. An advantage of some of these games is that youth with ASDs can focus on the task without having to interact with others very much, particularly if the games are computer based. A beginning list of ASD-friendly games and tips for using them is found at Autism Games (http://sites.google.com/site/autismgames/). The Autism Games website includes some of the following suggestions, which are applicable to all service providers, including librarians:

- Games should be a voluntary activity, not forced.
- Games should have an element of fun and be playful.
- Adults should control the materials and be involved.
- Games should match the child's capacity to succeed.
- Emphasis should be on visual, not verbal, interaction.
- Three rules of talking are to shorten sentences, to ask few questions, and to show what you mean.
- Adults should eliminate distractions.
- Participants should notice facial expressions, gestures, and body movements.

- Participants should respond to one another.
- Adults should make clear endings to the game and prepare for transitions.
- When the game becomes routine, incorporate new aspects.
- When it is not fun for someone, that person can stop playing.

DIGITAL TABLETS

Digital tablets, such as the iPad, are becoming learning tools of choice for youth with ASDs. Unlike typical assistive technologies, iPads and their counterparts are mainstream devices with a decidedly "cool" factor, which helps students feel accepted. In addition, the market is large enough to drive down prices, which is not always the case with assistive technology devices. The greatest impact for youth with ASDs seems to be on attention span; the format motivates individuals with ASDs to focus their attention and keep engaged in interactive activities. Tablets facilitate communication through alternative augmented communication apps as well as typing and drawing (which also help youth develop fine motor skills). At this point, iPad has a quarter million apps, several of which are targeted to people with ASDs. Service providers can also use the app IEP Checklist to track student progress. Librarians can research effective apps and provide lists for ASD service providers and families. The following are some helpful resources for finding apps:

A4cwsn.com (www.a4cwsn.com) reviews apps for children with special needs.

Apps for AAC (www.appsforaac.net/applist) lists nearly a hundred augmentative and alternative communication (AAC) language development apps, from AAC SpeechBuddy to ZenTap. Types of AAC apps include access, education support, eye pointing, Picture Exchange Communication System, photos and photo stories, phrase banks, set phrases, symbol grid systems, symbol sticks, text-to-speech, and word prediction. Note that this website is British.

Assistive Chat (www.assistiveapps.com) is an AAC app that includes key words, keyboard, and customizable text-to-speech.

Autism Epicenter (www.autismepicenter.com/TEST/autism-apps
.shtml) has rated dozens of useful apps; the highest-rated ones
are Pictello, Model Me Going Places (free), TouchChat, Prolo-
qu02Go, SLP Filed Kit, FirstWords, and Word SLapPs.

Autism Speaks (www.autismspeaks.org/family-services/resource
-library/autism-apps) has an extensive list of mobile apps for
youth with ASDs, ranging from ABA Therapy Images to Visual
Prompts Board. Its AACchicks site (www.autismspeaks.org/
docs/family_services_docs/AACchicks_Apps.pdf) also provides
a categorized list of their favorite apps. A third Autism Speaks–
affiliated group, Lovaas (www.autismspeaks.org/docs/apps_for
_autism.pdf), lists more apps by category.

AutismSphere (www.autismsphere.com) allows users to create a
customizable visual schedule.

Behavior Tracker Pro (www.behaviortrackerpro.com) helps quan-
tify behavioral process. The app can be used for taking notes,
and it can video record behaviors for later review. Input can
also be transformed into graphs and charts.

Conover Company's Functional Skills System (www.conover
company.com) provides a class set of iPods, functional skills
videos, and a management system.

Cookie Doodle (www.shoethegoose.com/CookieDoodle.aspx)
has users follow a recipe, simulate the cooking actions, and pretend to eat the finished product.

Interactive Technology Assisting Autistic Little Kids (www.itaalk
.org/images/iTaalk_Top_30_Starter_Apps_for_Special
_Education.pdf) offers its top thirty educational apps for less
than $50.

iTalk Lite (http://italksync.com) is a free app that turns the iPhone
into a recording device.

Kansas Instructional Support Network (http://kansasasd.com/
node/5581) lists many iPad applications for special education,
many of which are appropriate for youth with ASDs (e.g., First
Then Visual Schedule, iCommunicate, SoundingBoard).

Kindergarten.com (http://kindergarten.com) has several apps
(e.g., problem solving, rhyming, discrimination, emotions)

based on the principles of applied behavior analysis using a verbal behavior technique.

Lexia Primary Reading Program (www.lexialearning.com) helps children master basic reading skills, including beginning and ending sounds, syllables and segmenting, sight words, decoding skills, and vocabulary and comprehension skills.

Locabulary (http://locabulary.com) combines location and vocabulary to produce appropriate text-to-speech communication.

Model Me Going Places (www.modelmekids.com/community -social-skills-autism.html) helps children navigate in the community and contains a photo slide show of children modeling appropriate behavior.

Nuance (www.nuancemobilelife.com) has several appropriate applications for youth with ASDs, such as Dragon Dictation and the voice-activated Dragon Search.

Proloquo2Go (www.assistiveware.com/product/proloquo2go) is a customizable Picture Exchange Communication System.

See.Touch.Learn (www.brainparade.com) is an app based on applied behavior analysis and can complement formal ABA sessions.

Speak It! (http://future-apps.net/Speak_it!/Speak_it!.html) is a text-to-speech application.

Squidalicious (www.squidalicious.com/2011/01/ipad-apps-for -autism-spreadsheet-of.html) has a categorized spreadsheet of reviews and recommendations of iPad apps for autism.

Talking Tom Cat (and dog, bird, and giraffe) (http://outfit7.com/ apps/talking-tom-cat/) is a virtual pet cat that responds to touch and anything one says in a funny voice.

TapToTalk (www.taptotalk.com) turns an iPhone into an AAC device, and TapToTalk Designer customizes the app for children to create AAC albums.

Vicki Windman (2011) has listed a number of outstanding applications available from the Apple Store that are applicable to youth with ASDs (e.g., Super Why, to teach *wh* questions, such as who, what, and so on; Teach Me lessons for K–1; Everyday

Social Skills; Counting Bills & Coins; Kids Math; Telling Time; Pocket Phonic; Mee Genius).

Assistive Technology Hardware

As public institutions in general, and public schools specifically, have to comply with the growing number of legislative mandates to accommodate individuals with disabilities, the technological options have grown in response. Of course, technology as a whole has made great strides, which has benefited the general population and specifically those with ASDs. The following products all address the needs of youth with ASDs, and each has unique features:

DynaVox (www.dynavoxtech.com) communication devices include a range of assistive technology wands, tablets, and boxes that cost thousands of dollars. All of the devices help individuals communicate using computer-generated or recorded-speech output linked to the content available for users to stipulate. All devices support touch screens and alternative access methods (e.g., head tracking, switch scanning). Most have multilanguage capabilities, and some include word prediction.

Fusion (www.writerlearning.com/special-needs/fusion.php) is a keyboard and screen device that provides communication support through features such as word prediction, text-to-speech, speech augmentation, spelling help, keyboard instruction, writing prompts, math drills, instant feedback, and calendaring. Up to sixteen students can have individual protected workspace on the device.

GoTalk (www.attainmentcompany.com) is a message "tablet" that enables individuals to express preselected, customized recorded messages.

IntelliKeys (www.intellitools.com) is an alternative keyboard solution that works with overlays to help individuals communicate ideas.

Oklahoma's Assistive Technology Program (www.ok.gov/abletech/Assistive_Technology/Do_It_Yourself.html) provides directions for homemade assistive technology such as a soap-dish switch, a battery adapter, and a talking picture frame.

Speaks4Me (www.speaks4me.com) is an electronic communications and voice-output application device that allows users to
drag and drop images to a sentence strip to create a correctly
structured multiple-word sentence, which can then generate
speech.

Assistive Technology Software

As with hardware, the assistive technology industry has created hundreds of software programs that target specific ASDs issues and skills,
such as attention, social interaction, and language development. Some
software programs work well with most students, such as productiv-
ity tools or content-neutral programs such as flash cards. All kinds of
younger children can use the same software programs, such as Reader
Rabbit's Toddler. Teens with specific interests and skills may succeed
with higher-end software programs such as SketchUp. Just as the
library should have a rich print collection to address the diverse needs
and interests of its users, so too should the library provide a variety of
software that most clientele, including youth with ASDs, can use.

Librarians can help service providers evaluate software and find
vendors. MouseTrial has an extensive database of pay and free software companies that target this population (www.mousetrial.com/
autism_software_database.php). Cindy's Autistic Support (www.cindys
autisticsupport.com) is a directory of many free autism-support materials. Especially helpful are the visual technology resources.

Nowadays, software is seldom circulated, especially because many
products are downloaded online. However, the library can include
autism-targeted titles on its portal, along with resources for other targeted users. The following titles, most of which are not free, give an
idea of the variety of products available for youth with ASDs:

Activity Trainer (www.dttrainer.com) is a powerful software
program that makes the research-based, effective video-
modeling teaching method practical for the classroom and
home. The Activity Trainer is a versatile teaching tool that
enables teachers to use videos to teach almost any targeted
activity or skill—from simple to complex—and includes a library
of activities with options to customize, modify, and create new

activities. The Activity Skills Library provides hundreds of videos with still images, audio, text, and worksheet resources to teach hand-on skills, including academic, daily living, communication, social, recreation, and vocational. Many more activities are available as updates after purchase. Teachers can set up computer-based schedules for the students.

AutismTrack (www.handholdadaptive.com) is a portable (e.g., for use with an iPhone, iPad, or iPod Touch), customizable data tool that tracks behaviors and interventions and records diet, medicine, and therapy. It can be shared with the child's team.

Cogmed (www.cogmed.com) trains working memory.

Fluency Tutor (www.texthelp.com) tracks students' audio reading process and quizzes them to test reading comprehension.

Infogrip (www.infogrip.com) offers several software products that help children with literacy: Creature, Switch On, and Nouns and Sounds. ReacTickles help students learn technology and communication skills.

iPrompts (www.handholdadaptive.com) is a picture-based prompting app that holds thousands of images, and users can add their own pictures. It includes prompting templates (e.g., visual countdown timer, visual sequencer and scheduler) to help users transition and make choices.

Laureate (www.laureatelearning.com) sells two autism packages: one for emerging vocabulary to two-word combinations, and a second level that addresses early syntax and basic language mastery.

The National Library of Virtual Manipulatives (http://nlvm.usu.edu/) is based on ancient Chinese tangram blocks. The blocks can be dragged, rotated, and flipped to copy designs. The contents of this website are appropriate for math students across a range of categories of disability. It is available in English, French, and Spanish.

Readability (http://lab.arc90.com/experiments/readability) is a free, simple tool that makes reading on the web more enjoyable by removing the clutter around text.

Transporters (www.thetransporters.com) helps children with ASDs ages two to eight recognize emotions. The DVD package includes videos with five-minute episodes showing key emotions in context, interactive quizzes, and service provider guides.

VizZle (www.monarchteachtech.com) is a web-based interactive visual learning tool for individuals with autism. The product includes a library of premade lessons, learning objects, and templates for creating and customizing lessons. The software records student work and aligns with students' IEPs. The tools also include access to other peer-reviewed VizZle lessons.

Several text-prediction software applications help individuals with autism express their thoughts:

Co:Writer (www.donjohnston.com/products/cowriter/index.html) works with word-processing applications, including email and the Internet, to help poor writers and spellers produce grammatically correct and topic-specific sentences. The associated product Read:Outloud (www.donjohnston.com/resources/read outloud6_index.html) is an accessible text reader with embedded comprehension strategies.

Kurzweil 3000 (www.kurzweiledu.com) provides several scaffolds for reading: highlighted screen text, one-click access to word support, teacher-embedded "bubble notes" to help readers stay on track and comprehend text, word prediction, and audible spell-checker; it also enhances audible and visual access to web pages.

Read&Write (www.texthelp.com) offers a set of tools to help students read and write: word prediction, word checking, read-aloud function, dictionary, highlighting, DAISY reader, and student tracking.

Word Q (www.wordq.com) is a word-prediction program that works with existing word processing programs.

Visuals

Youth with ASDs are likely to learn visually, so images can act as effective cues for learning and transitioning. Visuals may be used as an augmented communication tool, cognitive scaffold, organization schedule, or behavior prompt.

A typical use is an individualized visual schedule, which shows a sequence of events, including possible changes or variations. A good practice is to laminate each image so the child can mark or otherwise indicate when he or she has finished with the activity. The sequence can refer to a library set of routines or the steps to accomplish a task, such as locating a book.

Similarly, social rule cards can be visual reminders of behaviors for specific situations, such as sitting at a table with other students in the library.

Images can help children make choices in terms of behaviors (e.g., alternatives to inappropriate behavior, choice of positive items).

The international symbol for *no* (red circle with a line drawn through it) is useful for communicating that an activity or items is not permitted.

Visual cards with stoplight symbols (i.e., green, yellow, red) can be used to facilitate transitions, such as prompting a child to finish up an activity. Other social transition cards can be used to indicate that a child should wait or take turns, or that a child needs help, has finished an activity, or needs downtime from an activity.

The Picture Exchange Communication System enables a child to give a picture of a desired item in exchange for the actual item. This process is useful not only because it helps those children with low-language development but also because it provides them with an opportunity to initiate communication, which can be challenging for them.

A set of cards with images can be used as conversation starters, such as "What books do you like to read?" Or photo albums can be used to help share past events or explain home life.

A "social story" relates a challenging social situation and teaches specific behaviors about interacting with others. It is written in the first person and has visual representations and text. The child can read it whenever he or she has the time and is calm. Similarly, a comic-strip conversation can illustrate social interactions. Videos can also help explain social situations.

The Mayer-Johnson software program Boardmaker offers a useful augmentative communication tool that is best conceptualized as a customized keyboard of images rather than letters. The choice of image used is important, though; the image needs to be clear and unambiguous. For that reason, a black-and-white line drawing may well be the most effective representation, even though it might be more abstract than a color photograph. Youth may be distracted by colors even in a simple color drawing (such as Boardmaker's Picture Communication Symbol) or may focus on incidental details in a photo, such as a toy in the background. Picture This (www.donjohnston.com/products/access _solutions/software/picture_this/index.html) is a good software program, which has more than five thousand photos without background distractions that can be used to generate cards with or without captions. In that respect, Dorling Kindersley illustrated books are usually comprehensible by youth with ASDs. For children who have difficulty understanding two-dimensional images, true object-based icons are a close representation of real objects because they are cut out in the shape of the actual item. Children with ASDs are sometimes early readers, but in any case, it is a good idea to include a printed label with the image and the word for it so that the child can start to associate the object or image with language.

Visual support tools can range from low to high technology. Low-tech solutions may consist of clipboards, whiteboards, image binders or albums, laminated cards (which may be collected on a ring), and highlighting tape to emphasize key words in a text. Low-end electronic devices include calculators, recorders, and simple voice-output devices. Higher-end technology includes laptops and other computers, adaptive hardware, and video cameras or playback systems.

Youth with ASDs sometimes use a portable set of visual cards, which the librarian should know about to optimize communication. In addition, librarians can create library-specific visual aids to post for all library users, not just those with ASDs. The librarian might also provide social stories for children to borrow or use at home before coming to the library or doing a new set of library tasks such as finding a book, conducting research, or listening to a podcast. This opportunity to rehearse expected behaviors helps mitigate the stress of new situations and serves as a preventative solution to possible frustration and meltdowns when a child is confronted with unanticipated change.

Avatars and Virtual Worlds

An avatar is a visual representation of a computer user. The avatar permits users to assume different identities through images of interest to them. Avatars have been used successfully with individuals with ASDs because the images are usually static or have limited emotional expressions, so they are easier to work with.

Some software programs use avatars as experts and guides, which lends a sense of personal connection between the user and the avatar. The avatar is often programmed to be patient and reassuring, even when users repeat the same actions for long periods of time. Individuals with ASDs particularly welcome such consistent support.

For some high-functioning youth with ASDs, the ordered experience of virtual worlds, such as Penguin Island, Whyville, SecondLifeKid, and Teen Second Life, provides a welcome alternative to everyday life. Communication can be conducted entirely by typing, movement is under users' control, and the avatars can circumvent the prejudices that some of these youth experience in school in that the features can resemble anyone or anything that the youth wants. Usually, the kids-only virtual worlds include monitoring features, which can intervene when inappropriate communication occurs.

The Center for BrainHealth in Dallas uses avatars that are stylized versions of their clients as a way for individuals with ASDs to learn social skills. The person interacts with other avatars in virtual-world simulated social situations. Being able to project the avatar rather than one's self is a safer feeling for individuals with ASDs, and they can rehearse appropriate behaviors repeatedly without negative repercussions.

Youth with ASDs often like locating and creating avatars for themselves when they interact with social media. The avatar images can be used a social cues to indicate personal interests while at the same time protecting their inner selves. Avatars can also provide some protection and anonymity for minors. Popular images include animals, cartoon figures, and objects. Here is a beginning list of avatar-generation programs that can be embedded in online environments (Terrile 2009):

> **Dollz Mania:** www.dollzmania.com (has several activities aimed at preteen girls)
> **Doppel Me:** www.doppelme.com
> **Gaia Dream Avatar:** www.tektek.org/dream
> **Lego Head:** www.reasonablyclever.com/blockhead

Otaku Avatar Maker: www.moeruavatar.com/index_en.shtml

Portrait Illustration Maker: http://illustmaker.abi-station.com/index_en.shtml

Visual Doll Makers: http://elouai.com/doll-makers.php

Yahoo! Avatars: http://avatars.yahoo.com (which requires a Yahoo! account)

RESOURCE MANAGEMENT

As librarians provide resources for youth with ASDs, they also have to think about how they will manage those resources for easy access and use. The overall physical arrangement, as well as the organization of information, needs to be addressed.

The library's collection of physical resources needs to be easily accessible by youth with ASDs and their service providers. The facility itself can support or impede the effective use of resources. To that end, the library environment should be as predictable as possible and should provide differentiated areas that meet the varied needs of youth with ASDs. For instance, quiet corners can calm highly sensitive children, and separate areas with colorful visuals and interactive learning stations can stimulate those who seek out sensory experiences. Furniture that focuses the child, such as carrels and separate computer stations, can lower distractions in the library. Chairs with "bumper" edges can help children orient themselves in their learning space.

To help youth not feel overwhelmed when trying to choose materials, particularly in a rich collection, librarians can code books that might interest youth with ASDs with colored labels or stickers. If these students participate in pullout activities that occur in a special classroom, librarians might consider checking out a set of relevant titles to the child's aide or education specialist to make available in that classroom a month at a time. Librarians can also create bibliographies of appropriate resources targeted both to youth and to their service providers; these lists can be provided in print and digitally, and they can be disseminated at events and via the library's web portal. As a further aid, librarians can add subject headings or other fields that indicate how a particular resource can be used or who it will be useful to.

As noted already, libraries tend not to circulate assistive technology because the items are often customized, such as programmed keys on a computer. Especially if youth use a particular tool throughout their education, that item tends to stay with them, and the family is responsible for keeping the technology in good order. However, some school libraries are responsible for site-specific equipment, in which case assistive technology can be checked out as needed: for a class period, overnight, or for the year. In any case, librarians should label all parts of the technology and check to make sure that it is in good operating condition when returned. If the technology includes cables and other peripherals, it is a good idea to keep all the pieces inside a sturdy container, such as a small suitcase, and include a checklist of the pieces along with instructions for connecting the pieces.

REFERENCES

Kahn, J., E. Middaugh, and C. Evans. *The Civic Potential of Video Games.* Boston: MacArthur Foundation, 2008.

Myers, B. "Minds at Play." *American Libraries* 39 (2008): 54–57.

Terrile, V. "Technology for Every Teen @ your library." *Young Adult Library Services* 7 (2009, Winter): 33–36.

Windman, V. " iPad Apps to Meet IEP Goals." *Tech & Learning,* May 25, 2011. www.techlearning.com/Default.aspx?tabid=67&entryid=293.

Wolfberg, R. *Peer Play and the Autism Spectrum.* Shawnee Mission, KS: Autism Asperger Publishing, 2003.

CHAPTER 5

Teaching Youth
with ASDs

LIBRARIES ARE BOTH FORMAL AND INFORMAL LEARNING ENVIRON-
ments. In all cases, librarians should find out which
youth have special needs and then gain basic knowledge about ways to create a suitable learning environment for them. Librarians increasingly focus on
intellectual access to information and ideas, so their
instructional role has correspondingly increased. In
that capacity, they need to find out which instructional
practices best fit which youth.

For youth with ASDs, instruction needs to be highly structured. Likewise, transitions between activities need to be explicit. Age-appropriate
and developmentally appropriate issues also need to be considered.
The appropriate course of action should include a curriculum adapted
by either resource teachers or other specialized teachers.

This chapter details effective instructional practices and includes
ways that librarians work instructionally with students with ASDs.

THE LIBRARIAN'S ROLE IN INSTRUCTION

Librarians want people to be effective users of information and ideas. To that end, librarians need to provide both physical and intellectual access to information. Particularly as libraries provide access to resources that librarians do not specifically select, librarians need to teach users how to evaluate resources.

Public libraries serve a broad spectrum of users, so their informal "curriculum" and their instructional mode vary greatly, from helping parents select board books for their children as part of a storytime event to Internet-searching workshops, from a tip at the reference desk to pointing out online tutorials. Few public libraries provide academic courses and programs per se; instead, they serve as effective informal learning centers. As such, they may offer onetime workshops or training in specific tasks, such as showing youth how to find a magazine article using a database aggregator. Thus, instruction tends to be modular, but it can be very responsive to an individual's immediate needs, which is a good fit for youth with ASDs who visit the library to explore their personal interests.

In contrast to public libraries, school libraries are formal instructional centers. To that end, school librarians may have a scope-and-sequence information literacy curriculum, or they may collaborate with classroom teachers on literacy standards. Because school librarians work with youth on a regular basis, they can build on prior instruction and their knowledge about a student. School librarians are also more likely than public librarians to teach groups of youth, and they often do much one-to-one instruction as well. Group instruction can be more time efficient, in theory, as all students get the same basic information and individualized help as needed.

Both public and school librarians might sponsor library clubs or interest groups, in which informal instruction might occur. Both types of libraries might offer trainings specifically targeted at groups of youth with ASDs. It should be noted, though, that even in such specific groups, behaviors and skills of the participants may vary widely.

SETTING UP THE PHYSICAL CONDITIONS FOR LEARNING

As mentioned before, the physical environment can affect learning for youth with ASDs. Fortunately, most libraries are structured, orderly environments (at least in the eyes of the library staff). Even so, youth with ASDs should be individually oriented to the space and shown around so that they can make sense of it. Particularly because youth with ASDs may have difficulties with self-control, the more that the environment is controlled, the more comfortable they are likely to be.

Simpson and Myles (1998) suggest several tips for making the physical space conducive to learning:

- Create clear physical and visual boundaries.
- Provide function-specific areas with minimal sensory distractions.
- Control the amount of light by using shades or blinds to create a calming atmosphere.
- Avoid fluorescent lights, and seat youth near natural light.
- Provide study carrels or other individual work spaces in a corner or area away from group-work areas.
- Reduce noise by using carpets, soundproofing tiles, and headphones if necessary.
- Provide simple, functional signage for labels, schedules, rules, and step-by-step instructions.
- Provide behaviorally based communication tools (e.g., picture-card files, social stories, portable assistive technology communication systems) in a fixed area.
- Provide activity-completion signals, such as "completed" boxes or pockets, choice boards or drawers (to choose an activity reward), or waiting supports such as a timer.

GETTING STARTED

Some general teaching principles for working youth with ASDs apply to librarians as well:

- Get to know each child.
- Try to address the full scope of deficits.
- Be sensitive to developmental sequences.
- Provide supportive teaching.
- Involve parents and service teams.

- Reduce the child's behavior that is incompatible with learning.
- Provide a predictable routine for programs and discipline.

These additional instructional strategies also work well for youth with ASDs (Maurice, Green, and Luce 1996; Shriver, Allen, and Matthews 1999):

- Select library materials on the basis of the child's interest.
- Use singing and rhythm activities to attract the child.
- Have the child sit closely to the instructional area.
- Have a predictable routine for activities: motivate, give clear goals, sequence processes, provide scripts for learning, use repetition, and remain patient and flexible.
- Limit distracting visual and auditory stimulation.
- Use speech and matching gestures simultaneously.
- Match instructional complexity with the child's comprehension level.
- Avoid "libraryese" and library idioms.
- Provide limited choices when appropriate.
- Give tasks, but omit one tool or supply to get the learner to ask for the item.
- Encourage trained peer interaction (buddying).
- Enhance response opportunities by using choral or group oral response and response cards (or handheld response systems).
- Give learners a silly situation to solve, such as how to read underwater.
- Take advantage of spontaneous learning opportunities by noticing the child's persistent gaze or engagement and talking with him or her about it.
- Discipline consistently and fairly.
- Redirect self-stimulatory activities with a new object or activity.
- To assist with transition, give warnings and visual cues before activities change.

INSTRUCTIONAL METHODS

Having a large repertoire of instructional strategies helps librarians choose an approach that matches the needs and strengths of youth with ASDs, and it enables librarians to make adjustments in response to how the youth react. When librarians teach large groups, the philosophy of inclusion holds, so as many people as possible respond positively and actively. Fortunately, librarians do much one-to-one instruction, and particularly because librarians are not the primary teacher, they usually do not have to focus on stretching the youth's learning styles.

Direct Instruction

Most youth with ASDs are comfortable with direct instruction. Step-by-step information in a logical sequence allows them to process things in an orderly way. Straightforward sentences, listed text, and visual cues help comprehension; in that respect, PowerPoint and other presentation tools help youth understand concepts. Youth with ASDs can be provided with study guides that consist of one slide and notes per page, preferably downloaded onto a laptop for the learner to use and adjust. Because youth with ASDs tend to be global learners, preferring to see the big picture, having a graphic organizer that shows that larger context is especially helpful.

Simpson and Myles (1998) suggest several direct instruction techniques for use with youth with ASDs. When setting up the learning activity, the librarian should select specific objectives for each person and plan a structured lesson. Librarians should briefly explain the personal benefits for learning the concept, such as learning to use an online library catalog to find a book on the person's topic of interest independently. The concepts should be presented at a brisk pace, with little downtime. Librarians should introduce some variety in the order of delivery for learners to have more opportunities for their sensory systems to process information actively. The can engage learners with content-related factual questions. The librarian should wait at least thirty seconds for responses. The librarian then can reinforce and model the correct responses, and give concrete examples to help learners connect the concept to their own lives. When learners can respond to questions 90 percent of the time, they are ready for independent practice.

Discrete Trial Training

In special education, the instruction method of discrete trial training (DTT) is often used with children with ASDs to teach skills that are best learned in small repeated steps. The DTT method also applies principles of behavior analysis to individual training in a systematic and controlled manner.

The DTT process is very structured (Bogin et al. 2010). The objective is set up with an antecedent, expected behavior, and criterion for assessing mastery; for example, the librarian asks the child to find a specific book, and the child then finds the correct book and shows it to the librarian 80 percent of the time asked. Next, the librarian conducts a task analysis of the skill, identifying and listing each step in sequential order. The steps need to be clear enough that any member of the child's team can do the training. Next, the librarian creates a data sheet to record the child's efforts each time, noting the date, setting, behavior, interfering behaviors, and criterion for mastery. The learning environment should be quiet, with few distractions. At this point, the librarian can actually start the trials. The trials should be massed, that is, repeated several times in a row so that "overlearning" occurs. It is important to select reinforcers for the task success, such as a desired object or enjoyable movement. Another aspect of DTT is discrimination training so that the child knows how to discriminate one stimulus from another, such as a fiction book from a nonfiction book.

Collaboration-Based Instruction

Because youth with ASDs tend to have social skill deficits, they often prefer to work independently. However, collaborative learning activities can not only help these youth become more socially competent and interdependent but also can leverage their strengths and supportively improve weaker skills.

Collaboration-based instruction consists of structured learning of academic and social tasks that require learners to work together to accomplish those tasks. Structural factors include heterogeneous small groups, distributed leadership, group and individual accountability, and group autonomy.

When teaching, librarians need to identify tasks that require several people working together, such as making a video or a magazine. Ideally, the task should call on several different roles or skills so that each person can contribute something unique while still letting all contribute; for instance, producing a newspaper requires interviewing, writing, layout, photography or artistic, and production skills. For younger students, contributions might consist of parallel skills and contributions, such as each child creating a page about an animal; this approach can be appealing to youth with ASDs who are more comfortable working alongside others than interacting with others, but such an approach may be better deemed cooperative rather than collaborative. Typically, a problem-solving approach lends itself well to collaboration-based instruction.

In collaboration-based instruction, the librarian needs to clearly define specific tasks and roles, assign groups, teach group-processing skills, monitor groups, and assess throughout the activity. Typically, the librarian introduces the activity with enough background information and direction for the students to explore and address a related topical issue independently. Basic group-processing skills include describing member roles, clarifying tasks, discussing the learning activity's issues and underlying factors, determining a strategy to achieve the activity's goal, working toward the goal, and assessing efforts in terms of content and social aspects (Johnson and Johnson 1997).

Social stories and task cards are useful ways to teach roles for youth with ASDs; theoretically, observing other students demonstrating the role is informative, but youth with ASDs tend not to mimic others or be motivated by others' actions (except when those actions negatively affect them). Because these youth tend to like routine, it makes sense to have the same group members in the same roles together for at least two projects, and to vary either group members or roles for the third activity so that youth with ASDs can experience some consistency and practice roles predictably. Typically, the librarian consults with the classroom teacher to assign group membership according to the mix of individual skills and knowledge. As with other activities, librarians need to signal upcoming transitions and prepare learners accordingly to prevent meltdowns.

Constructivist Instruction

In constructivist instruction, learners make meaning of their environment for themselves rather than passively absorbing the teacher's sense-making directive. As with collaboration, teaching largely consists of creating a learning environment, providing the resources needed to construct meaning.

Because constructivism builds on prior knowledge and the ability to make associations, youth with ASDs may exhibit uneven abilities learning this way. If the subject matter links to their existing interests, they may be able to excel and serve as an expert in small-group learning. The librarian or other teacher may have to supply the link between the topic and the child's interests to engage him or her.

Likewise, youth with ASDs can make connections between two concepts or sensory experiences. These connections are often very personal and might not resonate with others. For instance, the child may have seen a show about tortoises on the Galapagos Islands, so when a class discussion is about islands, the child might utter, "Tortoises!" Sometimes the associations can be visual; in fact, the well-known animal science doctor Temple Grandin (2006), who has high-functioning autism, asserted that some individuals with ASDs have a mental visual search engine that enables them to find patterns in numbers. In that respect, Google's image search engine can help all learners gain pattern-recognition skills.

However, developing new patterns can be difficult. Categories are the first step in forming a concept, according to Minshew, Meyer, and Goldstein (2002). These researchers found that people with ASDs can easily sort objects into preidentified categories such as "soft" or "hard," but they have difficulty thinking up other categories on their own for groups of objects. Librarians should work on teaching flexibility of thinking by playing a game that asks youth with ASDs to make up new categories for objects, like "objects containing metal" or "objects used in sports." Then the teacher should get the child to explain the reason he or she put an object in a specific category (Grandin 2006).

Constructivism may be approached as an individual or group learning activity. Depending on the concept, a learner with an ASD might succeed more easily doing the activity alone, without the distraction of other people and stimuli. In contrast, working with another person can help the learner make more connections.

The trickiest part of the whole process of constructivism is being open to the unanticipated conclusions that students make. If learners are supposed to arrive at an intended answer or concept using a variety of paths to get there, it might be difficult for youth with ASDs to meet that instructional goal. Such learners may come to their own original deductions. Particularly since some youth with ASDs have difficulty with cause and effect, they might reach the wrong conclusions. Piaget's developmental theory of learning, which focuses on the preoperative stage, highlights this phenomenon: young children tend not to understand the concept of conservation of volume, as when a tall, narrow vessel seems to hold more liquid than a wide, short vessel. Thus, librarians and other teachers should think about the ramifications of using a constructivist approach, and it may be that this strategy works best with older students.

MULTISENSORY TEACHING

Youth with ASDs often have sensory-processing deficits, which affect their ability to learn. However, these deficits are usually not across the board, so a youth with a deficit in one area, such as hearing, may have strengths in another area, such as high visual acuity. The challenge for librarians is to know about and address individual strengths.

Vision
Even though vision is often the preferred sense for learning for youth with ASDs, many youth may have issues with vision. For instance, they tend to rely heavily on peripheral vision, which can be more reliable than straight-ahead vision. They may have poor depth perception, and looking at colors or patterns may be physically painful experiences for them. Applin (1999) and Spiegel (2003) offer several techniques for optimizing visual components of instruction:

- Use simple, well-labeled handouts.
- Minimize visual distractions, such as dangling objects or visually busy walls.
- Use calming light and muted colors.
- Don't demand eye contact as a signal for attention; youth with ASDs pay attention without direct eye contact, which can be difficult for them. They are more likely to look at an object that is being discussed, such as a book, than at a person.
- Include visual hands-on experiences to explain an idea or skill.

- Avoid writing on a chalkboard or whiteboard while talking; if immediate writing is required, face the group and use an overhead projector or type onto a computer hooked up to the projector.
- Write in large letters in high contrast (black on white, or white on black).
- Place a black surface under worksheets.
- Use closed-captioning features when showing videos.
- Use pictures (including the Picture Exchange Communication System), to explain, not just for requests.
- Create cards with library-related vocabulary and accompanying images.
- Make library web pages accessible.
- Use a talking stick as a visual reminder about taking turns (the speaker holds the stick to talk).
- Use math manipulatives to teach number concepts.
- Incorporate "I Spy" and other visual-detail activities.
- Incorporate drawing into learning activities, such as using drawing to demonstrate what one has learned.

Other Senses

Other senses and sense responses can also distract youth with ASDs from learning. Moyes (2001) notes some specific sensory issues and ways for librarians to address them (noted in italic):

- Sound sensitivity to certain volumes or pitches so the learner may hum to drown out the sound. *Move the seat away from noise; apply felt to the tip of a chair leg; warn about coming noise; avoid using noisy equipment.*
- Touch sensitivity to light touch rather than deep-pressure touch, or might not be able to feel temperature or to deal with it well. *Provide a weighted vest as needed; let the person use instruments (e.g., grabbers) rather than hands (children tend to either love or hate finger painting).*
- Taste distortions and food preference and avoidance extremes, which are often due to food texture. *Avoid food in the library.*
- Olfactory sensitivity to certain smells, which can trigger negative reactions. *Avoid wearing perfume or perfumed lotions; avoid smells of smoke, as from a candle.*

- Difficulties in synchronizing to a rhythm or following the rhythm of a conversation. *Provide opportunities to play an instrument (e.g., tambourine, soft drums); encourage moving to music (a positive way to channel repetitive motion behavior); incorporate poetry and singing games; focus on participation rather than precision.*

Motor Skills Teaching

As noted before, youth with ASDs are likely to have deficient motor skills. At the same time, librarians can leverage such youths' sense of touch to optimize learning. Here are some aspects of motor skills deficiencies and ways that librarians can address them when instructing youth with ASDs (Furth and Wachs 1975; Notbohm and Zysk 2010):

Fine motor skills: play with puzzle pieces, such as of animals or buildings; learn the alphabet or the library classification system using cutout letters or by shaping clay; draw images by tracing stencils or templates; practice cutting skills; construct buildings using paper, boxes, blocks, clay, or software programs.

Movement based on visual focus: keyboard; draw dot-to-dots; solve visual puzzles.

Spatial relationships: construct models; work with blocks (especially with peers); read and create maps; construct and use topographical maps (especially bas-relief ones), create dioramas; solve spatial puzzles; fold paper (e.g., origami, maps, pop-up books); use a trackball rather than a mouse.

Body awareness: act out events and processes; copy movements for rhyming or singing games (e.g., "I'm a Little Teapot," "Itsy Bitsy Spider," "Lion Hunt"); act out animal movements; make the shape of letters using the whole body.

COMMUNICATION SKILLS

The heart of teaching and learning is communication: between the learner and content matter, between the learner and librarian, and between the learner and other learners. In some cases, youth with ASDs have average or even advanced language skills, but they may lack expressive skills. Even though librarians transmit and share content matter, they also address communication skills, which constitute part of information literacy.

The steps of communication illustrate this point well (implications for youth with ASDs are noted in italic). Librarians can focus on any of these steps in teaching youth with ASDs:

1. **A person has an idea.** The information-literate person generates ideas. *Youth with ASDs tend to think concretely and in terms of themselves, so they may need explicit instruction in making inferences, especially from different points of view.*

2. **The person externalizes that idea as a message.** The information-literate person chooses the medium and language to express an idea, based on the intended audience, circumstance, and so on. *Youth with ASDs tend to have difficulty speaking or writing for several reasons, such as limited vocabulary or problems with motor skills or sequencing. They may have unusual speech patterns and delays, loud or flat intonation, or a pedantic tone.*

3. **The person receives the message.** The information-literate person encounters information. *Youth with ASDs may have difficulties sensing the message, which means being aware of it, touching it, seeing it.*

4. **The person processes the message internally.** The information-literate person has the content and language background to make meaning of the information. *Youth with ASDs may have difficulty processing the message for several reasons: lack of vocabulary, lack of experience, neural problems, motor problems, emotional distractions, or physical ailments. As noted already, youth with ASDs tend to think literally, so they are unlikely to understand metaphors, irony or sarcasm, idioms, words with multiple or ambiguous meanings, or word play* (Notbohm and Zysk 2010).

5. **The person responds externally to the message.** The information-literate person chooses the medium, language, and action for responding. *Youth with ASDs may not see a reason to respond or may have difficulties expressing their response.*

As with other aspects of human growth, communication skills are developmental. Prizant and colleagues (2006) identified three stages of communication development:

1. **Social partner:** using gestures and vocalizations. These actions are usually accomplished in the first year of life. Youth with ASDs have difficulties with positive shared emotion and experience delays in learning how to signal intent. They tend not to initiate communication, which leads to fewer opportunities to learn how to respond. They also tend to pick up on aspects of communication signals that are not the critical feature of the action, such as an incidental scratching during a conversation.

2. **Language partner:** using symbolic means such as verbalized words or pictures to communicate shared meanings, which typically occurs between age one and two. Echolalia may occur that this stage as a transition strategy to contextualized conversation. Youth with ASDs tend not to observe others or monitor others' attention focus. They have difficulty learning through social observation and interpreting social cues. They also have a hard time recalling words outside of specific contexts, so they rely on gestalt language processing (i.e., whole language chunks) such as echolalia without comprehension or intent. They may also have physical difficulty in producing speech.

3. **Conversational partner:** extending social exchanges, becoming sensitive to others, and transitioning to conversational dialogue. These actions are typical of preschoolers, and at this stage, learning is based on instruction and collaboration. Youth with ASDs have difficulty using symbolic communication such as gestures, linguistic forms, and the appropriate use of objects that lead to imaginative play. They also lack awareness of social conventions across contexts.

Language Issues

Language is an issue for almost all youth with ASDs; even those with strong vocabulary may have a hard time decoding irony or ambiguity. Although many youth with ASDs appreciate well-structured language experiences—such as parsing grammar—thematic language activities that tie in to their own lives can offer them authentic experiences.

To begin with, librarians should work with the youth's service team to determine the youth's language comprehension (Quill 1995):

- What linguistic features facilitate comprehension, such as sentence length and structure?
- What speaker factors facilitate comprehension, such as tone of voice, repetition, gestures, and proximity?
- What contextual factors facilitate comprehension, such as motivation, routine, visual aids, concrete associations, and the choice of person?
- What routinized responses are used, such as echolalia, scripts, and perseveration?
- What developmental issues impede comprehension, such as abstraction ability?

Several linguistic issues can be problematic for youth with ASDs. Expressive language can be confusing in terms of semantics (contextual meaning) or pragmatics of situational use. Youth with ASDs tend to interpret language literally, so they may have difficulty with poetry, some forms of fiction, humor, and irony or sarcasm. They are likely to have problems with paralinguistics (e.g., stress, tone, picture to imply meaning), and typically use the same form of expression regardless of the situation, so that the same tone of voice might be used in a library and at a football rally or when speaking to a baby and to an adult. Likewise, youth with ASDs may have difficulty with extralinguistics, such as gestures to emphasize meaning, especially those youth who have poor body-space awareness.

Scaffolding can help youth learn appropriate language relationships. By lessening the cognitive load and breaking down processes into meaningful smaller steps, librarians and other educators can help youth with ASDs manage their learning and not feel overwhelmed. Of course, this approach has universal applications. Here are some ways to scaffold language learning and use (for more ideas, see chapter 6):

- Ask binary questions (e.g., "Did he eat a cake or a cookie?").
- Ask literal, discrete questions to enable youth to develop communication skills.
- Show how question syntax can be transformed into answer syntax (e.g., "Why do birds sing?" "Birds sing because . . .").
- Provide structured sentence templates, often encountered in second-language learning (e.g., "The dog runs in the yard," "The boy runs in the yard," and so on).
- Use worksheets, graphic organizers, and other prompts to guide language.
- Teach the *wh* questions (i.e., who, what, where, when, why, and how).
- Link words and images.
- Present information visually rather than orally.

Speech Issues

Speech can be particularly challenging for youth with ASDs. Notbohm and Zysk (2010) provide processes for beginning to advanced levels for helping youth create sound and become orally competent:

1. Practice deep breathing and exhaling, which help youth control their breathing patterns.
2. Practice producing vocalizations such as *zoom* or *whee*.
3. Practice intonation, such as variations in tone like whispering, questioning, and high and low.
4. Practice starting, maintaining, and stopping a sound reliably. Singing can be a useful strategy.
5. Strengthen tongue and articular muscles to distinguish *uh* and *ah* sounds (*ah* requires more muscle control) and other vowel sounds.
6. Develop consonant sound discrimination and articulation.
7. Sequence words.
8. Speak purposefully.

Notbohm and Zysk (2010) also offer step-by-step suggestions to help youth with ASDs converse with others:

1. Think about the person you will speak with. Consider their thoughts and beliefs.
2. Establish a physical presence. Find a comfortable and appropriate distance between you and the other person.
3. Observe the other person's actions and the environment. Pay attention to the words they use and their tone.
4. Use language to relate to the other person. Show interest in them and their actions.

It should be noted that youth with ASDs might avoid direct eye contact when speaking; they may feel more comfortable with peripheral vision or feel that direct eye contact is too intense or threatening for them. Some youth may have difficulty paying explicit attention to making eye contact and keeping up with a conversation. Although it is appropriate to tell such youth that most people expect eye contact because of cultural norms, it is probably better not to force the issue. Instead, a speaker can be positioned at or below the child's level, or can hold a desired object close to his or her own eyes for the child to observe and reach for. In the long run, communication skills are more important than eye contact.

Usually, librarians focus more on content than on developing children's speech habits. However, librarians can help children in this area by providing them with rich sound and speech experiences through nursery rhymes, word and singing games, poetry, storytelling, jokes, and readers' theater. Librarians can also incorporate sound experiences through musical instruments, audio and video recordings, and webcasting. Librarians should also be mindful of their own speech habits: they should speak clearly and enthusiastically, use the same terms consistently, and avoid long strings of verbal directions.

Dealing with Echolalia and Perseveration

Defined as the unusual repetition of words or phrases, echolalia may be triggered by an emotional stimulus or a stressful situation. It is more likely to happen in unpredictable or unstructured situations, and when a person has to accomplish a difficult or unfamiliar task. Echolalia can be either a step to more conventional communication or a pathological behavior that needs to be adjusted. Assessment is the key. Librarians need to determine the factors or triggers of the situation and what the individual experienced just before the echolalia occurred. What was the intent of the echolalia: to aid in interacting or self-regulation, or a means to draw attention to oneself or to resist (Prizant and Rydell 1993)?

Prizant and Rydell (1993) offer several strategies for minimizing or addressing echolalia:

- Structure and schedule instructional time.
- Modify and structure the environment to optimize a predictable purpose.
- Use a facilitative interactive style rather than a directive one.
- Simplify language.
- Respond to and promote communication intent.
- Wait for responses.
- Prepare for transitions.

Several strategies can be used to anticipate or stifle perseveration of echolalia, or the repetition of words or actions long after the associated stimulus has ceased. As with other characteristics of ASDs, when adults know the youth's areas of interests, they can consciously refer to or avoid the topic. Adults can redirect the youth's attention to another interesting stimulus or transition the interest to another related area of activity. Occasionally, perseveration is used to delay or avoid a challenging or negative activity; in this case, the adult needs to assure the person that supports are available to help him or her achieve success. Sometimes a preassigned buddy can help the individual stop his or her verbiage. For more advanced youth, adults may suggest that the youth write down their comments for further discussion at another time or in another venue; this approach is particularly effective with the use of Web 2.0 tools such as blogs.

In the long run, perseveration should be explicitly addressed because it can cause difficulties for the individual, particularly in social situations. For instance, if an individual uses perseveration to avoid tasks, an adult can train the youth to ask for help instead or to communicate discomfort with the task. Ideally, the person should self-monitor instances of perseveration. Videos provide objective evidence of perseveration, which the person can observe and then develop cues for avoiding the automatic reaction; a trained adult will probably be needed to help in this self-assessment and intervention. For example, the adult may help the youth identify the situation and create a cue to initiate a more appropriate behavior.

A Few Words about Augmentative and Alternative Communication

Youth with ASDs have wants like everyone else, and they depend on others to fulfill their wants, like everyone else. Youth with ASDs usually have language developmental delays, so they have more difficulty than other children their age expressing their needs so that another person can understand them and meet their request. An example is with babies: parents may well understand baby talk, but other people will be clueless. So too are families more likely to understand their relative with ASDs than others, but if a young person with an ASD is to lead a full life in society, then he or she can benefit from learning effective methods of communication.

Augmentative and alternative communication (AAC) is a scaffolded solution to help youth with ASDs communicate with others. Basically, AAC is an aid to communication: an aid or device external to the body to represent, select, or transmit messages (Mirenda and Iacono 2009). Usually, AAC is a visual language system, which may consist of terms and images communicated through hand signs (considered an unaided communication system), on a ring of flashcards, an augmented keyboard and computer, an interactive language board, a speech outlet, a mobile app, or another mechanism. The aim of using AAC is to enable individuals to interact and participate in activities of their choosing. The use of AAC can supplement or enhance written or spoken communication, but it should not hinder language development. Typically, these solutions lower people's psychological stress and help them to be more easily accepted by others.

Many AACs are available, including online resources. In some cases, AACs are targeted specifically to youth with ASDs, and other times they have a more general audience, such as learners with other special needs. Matching the AAC with the individual is key, and one must take into consideration communication needs and current capacities, such as language development, physical development, level of understanding, and interaction strategies of the user's frequent communication partners. Generally, low-capacity development typically requires a concrete object system: three-dimensional items that are similar to the intended object. Each kind of AAC requires training the child, so again, issues of cognitive or physical delays need to be considered. Furthermore, the youth's service team needs to help transition from AAC to more conventional language when possible.

The Picture Exchange Communication System (PECS) works for youth with minimal oral communication skill; as noted before, PECS is a set of images or three-dimensional parts of an item used to indicate intent, and the images are exchanged to obtain a specific goal. Voice-output communication devices translate the person's input (via words or images) into sounds; these programmed tools can be quite sophisticated and expensive.

Here is a beginning list of AAC options and resources:

The American Speech-Language-Hearing Association (www.asha
.org/public/speech/disorders/AAC/) lists organizations with
information about AAC.

Augmentative Resources (www.augresources.com) offers a variety
of mainly low-tech aids.

DynaVox (www.dynavoxtech.com) has a number of voice-output
communication devices that use either a dynamic display
system or an overlay system.

Tech/Speak (www.amdi.net) is a device that incorporates user-
inserted overlays; several companies make these types of tools
(e.g., AbleNet, Mayer-Johnson).

Visual Aids for Learning (www.visualaidsforlearning.com) develops and provides images to streamline and support independent communication.

A useful strategy for librarians is a library-specific placemat board. Using poster board, the librarian can create a semisyntactical vocabulary inventory so that youth with ASDs can work in the library more successfully. The librarian can then laminate and mount the poster board to make it sturdy, and store it in a readily available spot. The child points to each word and can get the desired item or make a comment as needed. Here is a starting sample grid:

PRONOUNS	NOUNS	VERBS	DESCRIPTORS	OTHER TERMS
I	book	read	more	please
you	computer	want	less	thanks
he	catalog	open	softer	yes
she	paper	done	larger	no

INTERACTION ISSUES

One of the main challenges for youth with ASDs is interaction. They tend to focus on their own needs, to think in terms of their own reality, and they are not particularly motivated by others. Some of this behavior has to do with difficulties in processing information and dealing with physical differences, such that they have less energy available to deal with others. Nevertheless, all communication is based on interaction, so youth with ASDs need help to communicate their own needs and to find ways to connect with others using language.

The first challenge is to get the youth's attention. Youth with ASDs tend not to look to others for signals about what do to, and they may be sensitive to touch. Therefore, librarians need to build natural reasons for youth to look at them, such as giving directions for providing resources that the child wants. Librarians can point to items of discussion, which provides a concrete focus for attention. For children to look into the librarian's eyes, the librarian can hold the object of interest close to his or her face. Youth with ASDs tend not to react to nuanced vocalizations, and they may respond in a relatively flat way, so that gestures work better for them to express emotion or emphasis. Slowed speech and repetition can help youth comprehend others and not feel overwhelmed.

Youth with ASDs may understand a concept or process, but they may not give the usual signals such as nodding, taking notes, or participating in class discussions. Responding can be challenging for youth with ASDs. For one thing, they may have difficulty coordinating their gaze, verbalizing, and gesturing. Handwriting can be difficult, so computer tablets can be a real boon. Generally, youth with ASDs are more likely to communicate when they are motivated and have some need that they want to be satisfied: asking for a booktalked title, wanting to get onto the computer, or needing to go to the bathroom. The intent is that the librarian can draw on students'—all students'—inherent interests when designing instruction or providing other library services.

Interaction refers not only to human interaction but also to interaction with the content and activity at hand. It should be recognized that attention does not equate intelligence, and youth with ASDs might not manifest outward signs of paying attention even though they are trying hard to process incoming information. Youth with ASDs tend to have a mental on-off switch so that they either sense everything, which can be distracting and hard to sort out, or they do not cue in. Visual sense is connected with concentration, so visual barriers can help a learner focus on the task at hand. The software program Play Attention includes a sensory-loaded helmet that can track children's attention movements as they direct the motions of on-screen characters; the program helps youth with ASDs concretely link visual attention with behavior. Librarians can help youth with ASDs interact actively with content in several ways, such as the following:

- providing all the tools for the learning activity
- encouraging engagement with the material at hand
- decreasing lower auditory distractions
- breaking down the activity into discrete, short-term steps
- providing the parameters for the learning task
- providing guidance to help youth begin the task, and then removing the prompt
- acknowledging that tuning out distractions can be challenging
- employing the "mand"-model procedure: noticing the youth's focus of attention, providing a mand (yes-no question), and

waiting for a response—then praising a correct response or modeling a correct response

LEARNING ACTIVITIES

Librarians should encourage youth with ASDs to be involved in library experiences alongside their peers, thus building on their strengths and interests. Technology can help learning by providing highly structured learning activities that can be repeated and paced according to individual needs, and it requires little social interaction. To help ASDs youth socialize, librarians should involve aides, such as by finding out which peer or aide is paired with the child and then having the aide sit near the librarian to reduce distractions or anxiety. Age- and developmentally appropriate issues also need to be considered.

As noted before, learning activities that build on students' interests and strengths are more likely to be engaging and meaningful. To optimize learning, a good strategy is to either use familiar and interesting content when teaching new processing skills or to introduce new subject matter using enjoyable and comfortable processing approaches. Because youth with ASDs are likely to make cognitive linkages unpredictably, librarians and other educators can scaffold those connections, which also models the concept of connecting ideas or processes. Librarians can also call on youth with ASDs to serve as subject or process experts as appropriate; the main difficulty in doing so, though, is probably channeling that knowledge and helping youth realize that others might not share their interest or have the time to develop high-level skills in the area. In either case, involving expert students help them develop social skills in the process.

Social Learning

Encouraging youth with ASDs to be learning experts demonstrates the potential power of social learning activities. Although learning can occur with little social interaction, much of learning is socially contextualized or constructed. Just as youth with ASDs can share their knowledge, they can also learn from their experienced peers. Particularly if another child shares a mutual interest, a child with ASDs may well accept coaching from that peer even more readily than from an adult. Furthermore, the act of teaching itself is a highly social experience, which can challenge even the most able person with ASDs.

Even apparently simple social tasks such as joint attention, sharing, and taking turns are important prerequisites and sometimes challenging skills for interactive learning and teamwork. Therefore, librarians can help youth with ASDs succeed when they teach them how to borrow and return books, and handle them respectfully. Listening to a story hour teaches all youth how to listen and to take turns talking. Standing in line, sitting at a table or in a ring, raising one's hand—these are social skills that all children practice in the library. Children with ASDs might learn these social skills in one setting, but might have difficulty transferring them to another setting, such as a library. School libraries provide a sheltered environment for these children to practice a variety of social skills outside the classroom. The public library is an open and largely accepting setting for youth with ASDs to practice social skills with strangers in the community under the supervision of a knowledgeable library staff.

Technology's Role

As noted in chapter 4, on resources, technology provides a wealth of learning options. Computers and other individual digital devices provided a one-to-one experience for youth with ASDs, which can help them focus and extend their attention span. Software programs can teach and reinforce concepts and skills with infinite patience, so that learners can listen to a story or test a skill repeatedly without the content quality being diminished. Interaction with these devices usually requires little communication skill, and for many users it can seem as if the technology were made just for them, which reinforces their worldview. Nevertheless, the Internet in particular enables learners to access information and to contact other people around the world, thus broadening their perspective. For youth who have limited physical coordination or control, assistive technology tools such as touch screens and trackballs can facilitate input, and augmented keyboards or writing-prediction software can facilitate meaningful language-based communication.

Giving an electronic tablet to youth with ASDs may engage them for hours—and minimize behavior problems—but little academic learning, at least in support of the intended curriculum, may occur. Indeed, some youth with ASDs might act out when facing an upcoming social learning activity, in the hope that they will be "relegated" to the isolated technology. Technology is not as appropriate as a learning tool when personal contact is needed, when certain motor skills need to be developed (even as simple as turning a book page), or when localized or time-sensitive content is being addressed.

Probably the most critical decision in instructional design is matching the technology with the learning objective and the child, with the child as the central point. It should be noted that technology, in this respect, includes hardware, software, and other digital documents. A good rule of thumb is to use the most stable, low-tech solution that enables the child to meet the learning outcome effectively. Here are some key factors to consider:

- Can the child physically manipulate the technology?
- Does the child feel comfortable with the technology?
- Is the child receptive to learning with the technology?
- Can the child operate the technology largely independently, with little monitoring (which can be a problem with the Internet)?
- Does the technology support the learning outcome?
- Does the technology support the content?
- Does the technology support skills for how to do something?
- Is the technology manageable in a mainstreamed environment with other people present and learning simultaneously?
- What is the time frame needed to learn to use the technology, and can the child meet the learning outcome in approximately the same time frame as the rest of the learners who use the technology?

Gaming

Games are a pleasurable way to enable youth with ASDs to develop skills in several arenas: body coordination, social interaction, pattern recognition, memory, and literacy. Some board and card games found to work well for children with ASDs and special needs include: Aggravation, I Spy (a memory game), Jenga, Pictionary, Sequence for Kids, and ThinkFun Zingo! Wii video games that are appropriate for this population include Active Life Outdoor Challenge, Boom Blox Bash Party, Cooking Mama World Kitchen, Hasbro Family Game Night 3, Just Dance 2, Part, Rayman Raving Rabbids TV Party, Sports, Sports Resort, and Super Smash Brothers Brawl (Wong and McGinley 2010).

In providing gaming programs, librarians should ensure a noncompetitive atmosphere with players at similar skill levels, which allows people to play at their own pace. A typical teen or adult volunteer or caregiver should accompany each child to provide opportunities for social interaction, especially with peer role models, and to monitor behaviors. Expectations need to be clear, and rules for playing, such as taking turns, need to be explained ahead of time and reinforced consistently.

Lesson Plans

The following websites include worthwhile lesson plans, many of which are targeted to youth with ASDs:

Do2Learn (www.do2learn.com) helps individuals with disabilities by providing learning tools and activities.

Interactivate (www.shodor.org/interactivate/) provides Java-based interactive math and science courseware.

Internet for Kids (www.internet4classrooms.com/special_needs _autism.htm) lists classroom and parent educational resources.

Kerpoof (www.kerpoof.com) enables youth to make drawings, pictures, cards, stories, and movies.

Love to Know (http://autism.lovetoknow.com/Category:Autism _and_Education) is a directory of resources, including lesson plans.

The National Lekotek Center (www.lekotek.org), a division of the Anixter Center, is a central resource on toys and play for children with special needs.

Poisson Rouge (www.poissonrouge.com/index_en.php) is a rich gallery of visually stimulating interactive activities for preschoolers, which older learners can enjoy as well.

Polyxo (www.polyxo.com) offers commercial curricula based on applied behavior analysis, floor-time techniques, and social stories.

Sandbox Learning (www.sandbox-learning.com) has resources for educators, including task analyses.

SEN Teacher (www.senteacher.org) provides free teaching and learning resources for students with special needs and learning disabilities.

Starfall (www.starfall.com) offers free and commercial phonics curricula and activities.

A Teacher's Town (http://ateacherstown.com/bburks/Interactive.html) has a directory of online games ("edutainment").

Visual Playlist (www.videoplaylist.org) enables users to create a private video playlist, which is accessible from anywhere.

Zac Browser (www.zacbrowser.com) is an Internet browser designed specifically for children with ASDs, and the company provides community-based apps, including games, activities, and videos.

Zimmer Twins (www.zimmertwins.com) and **Xtranormal** (www.xtranormal.com) are simple tools for making animated movies and a fun way to create stories that help build social skills.

ASSESSMENT

The concept of assessment is complex with respect to ASDs because the term can be applied to diagnostics about different aspects of development, available resources and constraints, and other people who support the youth, as well as attitudes, motivations, and behavior. This section addresses only assessment of academic achievement, or testing.

This book has addressed the issue of equity throughout. Youth with ASDs should have equitable access to resources and equitable learning experiences. Although these youth have developmental delays, education should not be "dumbed down" for them. Rather, age- and developmentally appropriate considerations and modifications should be made so that youth with ASDs can experience essentially the same curriculum and material as other students do. Likewise, youth with ASDs should be encouraged to perform competently, reflecting their capabilities as accurately as possible.

Curriculum-based assessment helps determine the learner's knowledge, procedural skill, academic progress, and learning gaps. For youth with ASDs, frequent short-duration assessments that are sensitive to progress over time are an effective strategy. In this way, specific interventions can be introduced in a timely way for learners to repeat until they are comfortable and capable (Hall 2009).

Dealing with testing can seem tricky, as it requires balancing reasonable accommodations with proscribed educational standards. Sometimes what is measured is not the intent of the instruction; for instance, a writing portfolio may measure a person's ability to organize or self-reflect more than it measures writing ability. Therefore, careful attention needs to be paid to determine exactly the content and type of learning that is intended. Some of the usual accommodations considered for learners with special needs, including youth with ASDs, follow:

- extended time
- administration of assessment over time (broken down into several sections)
- separate location or specialized setting
- alternative modalities for communicating competency, such as keyboarding or using images
- use of assistive technology
- choice of prompts to answer
- assessment of fewer or only essential learning outcomes
- unique contribution to a group project
- holistic assessment of authentic performance
- portfolio of selected work over time

It should be noted that the context of the testing measurement can significantly skew results, because many youth with ASDs are hypersensitive to their surroundings or easily distracted (Hall 2009). Therefore, the testing conditions also need to be considered: the learning environment itself (e.g., facilities, furniture, lighting, sound), the people in the setting, the assessment materials, and timing issues.

CONCLUDING THOUGHTS

Whatever the activity, librarians need to think about learners' developmental stages. How advanced is their language skill? How social are they? What is their emotional response level? What is their physical development? What prior knowledge and experiences do they bring? These same questions apply to all learners, but they are especially important in working with youth with ASDs because their development tends to be atypical in comparison with that of others who are of the same age. Nevertheless, humans are social animals, and even the most isolated youth with ASDs lives in the midst of others and needs the opportunity to interact with others in age-normative ways. Thus, social issues such as body self-consciousness and cliques, which become more important in middle school, need to be acknowledged when providing meaningful library experiences. For example, *Goodnight Moon,* by Margaret Brown (Harper & Row, 1947) might meet a particular middle schooler's need for language skills development, but it is not relevant for most middle schoolers no matter their capability.

Nor does the librarian exist alone in the teaching role. Simpson and Myles (1998) offered a useful collaborative model that can serve as a way to think about teaching and learning in general. They asserted that four areas need to be addressed collaboratively to ensure the successful inclusion and learning success for youth with ASDs:

1. The learning environment and curriculum need to be modified, and general educational classroom (including library) support must be provided.
2. Attitudinal and social support must be available.
3. An ASD team needs to be committed and coordinated.
4. Home-library (and school) collaboration is necessary.

REFERENCES

Applin, M. "Instructional Services for Students with Disabilities." *Journal of Academic Librarianship* (1999): 139–41.

Bogin, J., L. Sullivan, S. Rogers, and A. Stabel. *Steps for Implementation: Discrete Trial Training.* Sacramento, CA: National Professional Development Center on Autism Spectrum Disorders, 2010.

Furth, H., and H. Wachs. *Thinking Goes to School: Piaget's Theory in Practice.* New York: Oxford University Press, 1975.

Grandin, T. *Thinking in Pictures.* New York: Vintage Press, 2006.

Hall, L. *Autism Spectrum Disorders: From Theory to Practice.* Upper Saddle River, NJ: Merrill, 2009.

Johnson, D., and R. Johnson. *Learning Together and Alone.* 4th ed. Needham Heights, MA: Allyn & Bacon, 1997.

Maurice, C., G. Green, and S. Luce, eds. *Behavioral Intervention for Young Children with Autism: A Manual for Parents and Professionals.* Austin, TX: Pro-Ed. 1996.

Minshew, N., J. Meyer, and G. Goldstein. "Abstract Reasoning in Autism: A Disassociation between Concept Formation and Concept Identification." *Neuropsychology* 16 (2002): 327–34.

Mirenda, P., and T. Iacono. *Autism Spectrum Disorders and AAC.* Baltimore: Paul H. Brookes, 2009.

Moyes, R. *Incorporating Social Goals in the Classroom.* London: Jessica Kingsley Publishers, 2001.

Notbohm, E., and V. Zysk. *1001 Great Ideas for Teaching and Raising Children with Autism or Asperger's.* 2nd ed. Arlington, TX: Future Horizons, 2010.

Prizant, B., and P. Rydell. "Assessment and Intervention Considerations for Unconventional Verbal Behavior." In *Communicative Approaches to the Management of Challenging Behavior,* edited by J. Reichle and D. Wacker, 263–97. Baltimore: Paul H. Brookes, 1993.

Prizant, B., A. Wetherby, E. Rubin, A. Laurent, and P. Rydell. *The SCERTS Model.* Baltimore: Paul H. Brookes, 2006.

Quill, K. *Teaching Children with Autism.* New York: Delmar, 1995.

Shriver, M., K. Allen, and J. Matthews. "Effective Assessment of the Shared and Unique Characteristics of Children with Autism." *School Psychology Review* 28 (1999): 538–58.

Simpson, R., and B. Myles, eds. *Educating Children with Autism: Strategies for Effective Practice.* Austin, TX: Pro-Ed, 1998.

Spiegel, B. *Helping Children with Autism Learn.* New York: Oxford University Press, 2003.

Wong, P., and A. McGinley. "Rated E for Everyone." *School Library Journal* 56 (2010): 22–23.

CHAPTER 6

Focus on Reading

JUST AS THERE IS NO ONE WAY TO DEFINE A CHILD WITH AN ASD, THERE IS NO one way to define a reader with an ASD. All of the following behaviors reflect experiences of youth with ASDs who read:

- John prefers nonfiction because fiction forces his thoughts to go beyond the literal.
- Michael loves Harry Potter and has read the series repeatedly.
- Sean runs around the room when the librarian is telling the story, but he understands it.
- Karen has read all of the library's biographies.
- Miguel rocks gently while poetry is read aloud.
- Tommy enjoys punching his favorite phrase on a story available on the iPad, where the VoiceOver app provides a gesture-based screen reader.

Reading is a core element of libraries in terms of providing worthwhile materials (in more formats than ever) and helping users enjoy the reading experience. Youth with ASDs often have language difficulties and can find comprehension a challenge, yet reading can be a preferred way for them to learn because written words are static and are easier to focus on than oral language. More generally, youth with ASDs need to become literate, and they should also have opportunities to experience and enjoy recorded language.

This chapter focuses on resources and services related to reading for youth with ASDs. It also addresses reading issues such as hyperlexia, a syndrome observed in children who have the precocious ability to read words. As with other issues, librarians should use a team approach to reading by working with a youth's peers, teachers, support personnel, and families.

READING RESOURCES

Librarians try to discover their users' interests as they acquire reading materials for the library, and the interests of youth with ASDs are no exception. Librarians should also seek the advice and suggestions of youth with ASDs for acquiring materials (it is important to follow up on those suggestions because youth may expect all the titles to be acquired and loaned to them). Besides the unique passions of each child, some other areas appeal to this population in general. For instance, both fiction and nonfiction accounts of youth with ASDs resonate and help these youth feel less isolated or different. Autism Asperger Publishing Company, Future Horizons, Jessica Kingsley, Paul H. Brookes, RainChild Network, and Woodbine House have published many books on ASDs for all ages. The following sites provide bibliographies of titles that may be of interest to or apply to youth with ASDs and their service providers:

> **Association for Library Service to Children** (www.ala.org/ala/ mgrps/divs/alsc/confevents/alscannual/bibliographyrecs .pdf), a list of recommended books about ASDs by expert Dr. Ricki G. Robinson
> **AutMount** (www.autmont.com/2011/03/graphic-novels-for -kids-with-autism.html), a site that provides autism information, events, and community serving Montgomery County, Maryland

Be a Good Dad (www.beagooddad.com/237/good-books-for
-children-with-autism/), a blog with posts about family issues
surrounding ASDs

Books for Children with Autism (www.autismreads.com), a site for
finding and suggesting books for children with autism and for
discussing ASDs

Children's Autism Books (www.autism-resources.com/books
-children.html), an annotated alphabetical list of fiction
and nonfiction books geared to children

Libraries and Autism (www.librariesandautism.org), a website
with resources to help library staff serve individuals with
ASDs and their families

Lovetoknow Autism (http://autism.lovetoknow.com/Kids
_Magazine_for_Autistic_Children), resources for mothers
of children with ASDs

Explaining ASDs

The following books are useful for explaining ASDs to youth with
ASDs, their peers, families, and other adults:

BOOKS FOR YOUNGER CHILDREN

Altman, A. *Waiting for Benjamin*. Tarrytown, NY: Albert Whitman,
2008.

Bleach, F. *Everyone Is Different*. Overland Park, KS: Autism Asperger
Publishing, 2002.

Clark, J. *Jackson Whole Wyoming*. Overland Park, KS: Autism Asperger
Publishing, 2005.

Day, A. *The Flight of the Dove*. New York: Farrar, Straus & Giroux,
2004.

Edwards, B., and D. Armitage. *My Brother Sammy Is Special*. New
York: Sky Pony Press.

Ellis, M. *Keisha's Doors / Las puertas de Keisha*. Austin: Speech Kids
Texas Press, 2005.

Ely, L. *Looking after Louis*. Tarrytown, NY: Albert Whitman, 2004.

Gaynor, *A Friend Like Simon*. New York: Special Stories, 2009.

Keating-Velasco, J. *A Is for Autism, F Is for Friend*. Overland Park, KS:
Autism Asperger Publishing, 2007.

Lears, L. *Ian's Walk*. Park Ridge, IL: Albert Whitman, 1998.

Moore-Mallinos, J., and M. Fabrega. *My Brother Is Autistic.* Hauppauge, NY: Barron's, 2008.

Murrell, D. *Friends Learn about Tobin.* Arlington, TX: Future Horizons, 2007.

Peete, H. *My Brother Charlie.* New York: Scholastic, 2010.

Sabin, E. *The Autism Acceptance Book.* New York: Watering Can, 2006.

Shally, C., and D. Harrington. *Since We're Friends: An Autism Picture Book.* New York: Sky Pony Press, 2012.

Thompson, M. *Andy and His Yellow Frisbee.* Bethesda, MD: Woodbine House, 1996.

Tourville, A. *My Friend Has Autism.* Mankato, MN: Magination, 2010.

Wilson, L. *Autistic? How Silly Is That!* Arlington, TX: Future Horizons, 2012.

Yamanaka, L., and A. Jasinsk. *The Heart's Language.* New York: Hyperion, 2005.

BOOKS FOR CHILDREN AGE TEN AND OLDER

Barraclough, S. *I Know Someone with Autism.* Chicago: Heinemann-Raintree, 2011.

Baskin, N. *Anything but Typical.* New York: Simon & Schuster, 2009.

Choldenko, G. *Al Capone Does My Shirts.* New York: Dial, 2006.

Crowley, S. *The Very Ordered Existence of Merilee Marvelous.* New York: Greenwillow, 2007.

Dowd, S. *London Eye Mystery.* Oxford, UK: David Fickling, 2007.

Duane, D. *A Wizard Alone.* Orlando, FL: Magic Carpet Books, 2003.

Erskine, K. *Mockingbird.* New York: Philomel, 2010.

Hoopmann, K. *Blue Bottle Mystery: An* Asperger Adventure. London: Jessica Kingsley, 2000.

Kochka. *The Boy Who Ate Stars.* New York: Simon & Schuster, 2006.

Lord, C. *Rules.* New York: Scholastic, 2006.

Martin, A. *Kristy and the Secret of Susan.* New York: Scholastic, 1990.

Matlin, M., and D. Cooney. *Nobody's Perfect.* New York: Simon & Schuster, 2007.

Rodowsky, C. *Clay.* New York: Farrar, Straus, & Giroux, 2001.

Tarshis, J. *Emma Jean Lazarus Fell out of a Tree.* New York: Dial, 2007.

Verdick, E., and E. Reeve. *The Survival Guide for Kids with Autism Spectrum Disorders (and Their Parents).* Minneapolis, MN: Free Spirit, 2012.

BOOKS FOR TEENS

Atwood, M. *Living with Autism*. Minneapolis, MN: Essential Library.

Bonnice, S. *The Hidden Child: Youth with Autism*. New York: Mason Crest, 2004.

Cain, B. *Autism, the Invisible Cord: A Sibling's Diary*. Mankato, MN: Magination, 2012.

Dooley, S. *Livvie Owen Lived Here*. New York: Feiwel and Friends, 2010.

Franklin, E., and B. Halpin. *The Half-Life of Planets*. New York: Hyperion, 2010.

Geus, M. *Piggy*. Honesdale, PA: Front Street, 2008.

Haddon, M. *The Curious Incident of the Dog in the Night-Time*. New York: Doubleday, 2003.

Hoopmann., K. *Haze*. London: Jessica Kingsley, 2003.

Kelly, T. *Harmonic Feedback*. New York: Holt, 2010.

O'Toole, J. *The Asperkid's (Secret) Book of Social Rules*. London: Jessica Kingsley, 2012.

Roy, J. *Mindblind*. Tarrytown, NY: Marshall Cavendish, 2010.

Stork, F. *Marcelo in the Real World*. New York: Scholastic, 2009.

Werlin, N. *Are You Alone on Purpose?* Boston: Houghton Mifflin, 1994.

BOOKS FOR TEENS WRITTEN BY TEENS WITH ASDS

Ginsberg, B. *Episodes: My Life As I See It*. New York: Roaring Brook Press, 2009.

Jackson, L. *Freaks, Geeks & Asperger Syndrome: A User Guide to Adolescence*. London: Jessica Kingsley, 2002.

Kraus, J. *The Aspie Teen's Survival Guide*. Arlington, TX: Future Horizons, 2012.

Price, J., and J. Fisher. *Take Control of Asperger's Syndrome: The Official Strategy Guide for Teens with Asperger's Syndrome and Nonverbal Learning Disorder*. Waco, TX: Prufrock, 2010.

Sicile-Kira, C., and J. Sicile-Kira. *A Full Life with Autism*. New York: Palgrave Macmillan, 2012.

BOOKS ABOUT ASDS FOR ADULTS

Attwood, T. *The Complete Guide to Asperger's Syndrome*. London: Jessica Kingsley, 2008.

Doyle, B., and E. Iland. *Autism Spectrum Disorders from A to Z.* Arlington, TX: Future Horizons, 2004 (also available in Spanish).

Notbohm, E. *Ten Things Every Child with Autism Wishes You Knew.* Arlington, TX: Future Horizons, 2005.

Riley-Hall, E. *Parenting Girls on the Autism Spectrum.* London: Jessica Kingsley, 2012.

Rogers, S., G. Dawson, and L. Vismara. *An Early Start for Your Child with Autism.* New York: Guilford, 2012.

Sastry, A., and B. Aquirre. *Parenting Your Child with Autism.* Oakland, CA: New Harbinger, 2012.

Shore, S., and L. Rastelli. *Understanding Autism for Dummies.* New York: Wiley, 2006.

Winslet, K., and M. Ericsdottir. *The Golden Hat: Talking Back to Autism.* New York: Simon & Schuster, 2012.

Books for Youth with ASDs

Certain literary features tend to resonate with youth with ASDs. In general, predictable books appeal to them. For older readers, formulaic stories and series work well. Youth with Asperger's syndrome are more likely to read chapter books or more advanced texts, whereas youth with moderate to severe ASDs read nonfiction and also enjoy just looking at the pictures. Two good lists of predictable titles are found at Loudon County (Virginia) Public Library (http://library.loudoun.gov/Default.aspx?tabid=85) and at the website Goodreads (www.goodreads.com/shelf/show/prediction-books). More specific devices and types of stories that appeal to these young readers follow:

> **Chain or circular stories:** The plot is interlinked so that the end leads back to the beginning (e.g., *If You Give a Mouse a Cookie,* by Laura Numeroff, HarperCollins, 1985).
>
> **Cumulative stories:** Each time a new event occurs, all previous events are repeated in order (e.g., *I Know an Old Lady,* by Charlotte Zolotow, Greenwillow, 1992).
>
> **Familiar sequence:** The writing is organized by recognizable theme, such as days of the week (e.g., number books, alphabet books).
>
> **Change books:** The book tells about how things develop and change (e.g., seasons, Change series, by S. M. Stirling)

Yesterday, today, and tomorrow books. These books help teach time sense (e.g., *Time to . . .*, by Bruce McMillan, Scholastic, 1989).

Pattern stories: Scenes are repeated with some variation (e.g., *Brown Bear, Brown Bear*, by Bill Martin, Holt, Rinehart and Winston, 1983).

Question and answer: The same or similar question is repeated (e.g., *Are You My Mother?*, by Philip Eastman, Random House, 1960).

Repetition of phrase: The word order in a phrase is repeated (e.g., *The Very Busy Spider*, by Eric Carle, Philomel, 1984).

Rhyme (e.g., books by Dr. Seuss).

Songbooks (e.g., *Wee Sing*, by Pamela Beall, Price/Stern/Sloan, 1983).

Motor-skills books (e.g., flap and sticker books).

Visual discrimination: Look and find images (e.g., *Where's Waldo?*, by Martin Handford, Little, Brown, 1987).

Motor planning: Each book tells how to do something step by step (e.g., I Can Draw series, by Walter Foster Publishing).

Nonfiction and realistic fiction are usually more successful than poetry or abstract writing because youth with ASDs tend to be literal, concrete thinkers. Likewise, books with clear photographs, such as reference books published by Dorling Kindersley, provide context-free images that are easier to understand. Large-format coffee-table books are great; carrying them often meets a youth's need for sensing heaviness, and the pictures are the only text youth need to understand. Graphic novels (especially nonfiction titles) with low reading levels are another visual option for advanced youth. Newspapers can also be great reading sources for youth with ASDs, especially allowing them to focus on specific interests, such as sports statistics, weather, or cartoons. Of course, sharing more fanciful and lyrical writing can also help these youth comprehend and appreciate these genres. Irony and wordplay might be lost on youth with ASDs, so instances of these writings need to be explained to them. An interesting activity, which can engage all learners, is to explore idioms and their origins, such as "dressed to the nines."

This starting list of books works well with children who have ASDs:

Baer, G. *Thump, Thump, Rat-a-Tat-Tat.* New York: HarperCollins, 1992.

Boynton, S. *Hippos Go Berserk!* New York: Little Simon, 2000.

Briggs, R. *The Snowman.* New York: Penguin, 2002.

Bunting, E. *Flower Garden.* New York: Harcourt, 1994.

Carle, E. *Rooster's Off to See the World.* Lancaster, PA: Childcraft Education, 1997.

Cousins, L. *Maisy Big, Maisy Small.* Somerville, MA: Candlewick Press, 2007.

Cronin, D., and B. Lewin. *A Barnyard Collection.* New York: Atheneum, 2010.

Duff, M. *Rum Pum Pum.* New York: Macmillan, 1978.

Dunbar, J. *Seven Sillies.* New York: Red Fox, Random House, 1999.

Dunphy, M. *Here Is the Southwestern Desert.* Berkeley, CA: Web of Life Children's Books, 2007.

Ehlert, L. *Growing Vegetable Soup.* New York: Harcourt, 1987.

Fleming, D. *In the Tall, Tall Grass.* New York: Henry Holt, 1993.

Galdon, P. *The Old Woman and Her Pig.* New York: McGraw-Hill, 1960.

Guarino, D. *Is Your Mama a Llama?* New York: Scholastic, 1989.

Hall, Z. *It's Pumpkin Time.* New York: Scholastic, 1996.

Hockerman, D. *Great Big Turnip.* Morristown, NJ: Silver, Burdett, and Ginn, 1989.

Horacek, P. *Butterfly, Butterfly.* Cambridge, MA: Candlewick, 2007.

Krauss, R. *The Carrot Seed.* New York: HarperCollins, 2004.

Maris, R. *Are You There, Bear?* New York: Puffin, 1986.

Martin, B. *Chicka Chicka Boom Boom.* New York: Beach Lane, 2011.

McGrath, B. *The M&M's Brand Counting Book.* Watertown, MA: Charlesbridge, 2002.

Numeroff, J. *If You Give a Moose a Muffin.* New York: HarperCollins, 1994.

Rothman, C. *I Love Snow.* Cinnaminson, NJ: Newbridge Communications, 1993.

Savage, S. *Where's Walrus?* New York: Scholastic, 2011.

Sendak, M. *Where the Wild Things Are.* New York: Harper & Row, 1963.

Seuss, Dr. *Dr. Seuss's ABC.* New York: Random House, 1991.

Shaw, N., and M. Apple. *Sheep Blast Off!* San Anselmo, CA: Sandpiper Press.

Sheppard, J. *Splash! Splash!* New York: Macmillan, 1994.

Smith, M., and A. Frase. *Point to Happy.* New York: Workman, 2011.

Thomas, J. *Can You Make a Scary Face?* New York: Beach Lane, 2009.

Tullet, H. *Press Here.* San Francisco: Chronicle Books, 2011.

Walsh, E. *Balancing Act.* New York: Beach Lane, 2011.

Ward, C. *Cookie's Week.* New York: Puffin, 1997.

Weisner, D. *Tuesday.* New York: Clarion, 1991.

Willems, M. *The Pigeon Wants a Puppy!* New York: Hyperion, 2008.

Wood, A. *The Napping House.* New York: Harcourt, 1984.

Wood, J. *Moo Moo, Brown Cow.* New York: Harcourt, 1992.

Yolen, J., and M. Teague. *How Do Dinosaurs Count to Ten?* New York: HarperCollins, 2009.

Ziebert, H. *Swim Buddies.* Maplewood, NJ: Blue Apple Books, 2006.

Zolotow, C. *Summer Is . . .* Morristown, NJ: Silver, Burdett, and Ginn, 1991.

Wordless books (e.g., *Zoom,* by Istvan Banyai, Puffin, 1998) and movies (e.g., *The Red Balloon,* by Albert Lamorisse, Doubleday, 1978) can also work well with youth with ASDs because the images carry the story. Notbohm and Zysk (2010) suggested several ways to share wordless books:

- Use the cover as a means to predict aspects of the story.
- Before turning a page, ask how the next page might differ, to develop prediction skills.
- Ask questions (who, what, where, when, why, how).
- Sequence the pictures logically.
- Make up a story.
- Make up character names.
- Explore feelings by interpreting characters' body language.

Physical Features of Books for Youth with ASDs

The reading experience also includes the physicality of the reading material. When choosing which version of a book to purchase, librarians should consider the following features:

Books that lie flat. Books that have to be held with both hands can be difficult to handle; spiral books usually stay flat.

Board books. These and other books with stiff pages are easy to turn.

Books with real photographs. Youth with ASDs tend to think literally. They can connect the pictures in the book with the real world. Children understand pictures that are symbols of real objects. Easy-to-identify photographs get children's attention and keep them motivated to stay engaged. For example, the illustrations in Dorling Kindersley reference books are easier to decipher than more abstract images.

Books with multisensory features. Nonreaders can interact with books that have texture, raised features, sound, lights, or scratch-and-sniff.

Books with props. Items such as train models and train sounds go along with *Thomas the Tank Engine* (a favorite for many children with autism).

In addition, there are several techniques to make books more accessible:

- Laminate pages to make them stiffer and easy to turn.
- Put paper clips on the corners of pages to help children turn pages.
- Apply different textures to books for multisensory appeal: sandpaper, cotton, velvet, bubble wrap.
- Outline images and text using puff paint.
- Use large-type formats.
- Use graphic versions of stories.
- Use the text-to-speech feature on computers to read online materials.
- Use the AutoSummarize feature in Microsoft Word to automatically extract the main parts of a text.
- Complement the text with sound effects, or pair a book with its audio version.
- Use e-books.
- Have the child record reading the book aloud using a computer or audiocassette. He or she can listen to the reading and repeat the process until satisfied with the results and until he or she knows the story.
- Supplement books with visual dictionaries.
- Offer a reading buddy.

READING ISSUES

Although most librarians are not reading specialists, those who serve youth with ASDs should have a sense of how these youth interact with reading materials. This knowledge can help librarians provide a more effective reader's advisory service and just-in-time friendly reading tips to help youth understand textual information.

What Makes a Good Reader?

Reading can be a whole-body experience. Reading requires focused attention. The eyes sense the text and record it to the visual cortex of the brain. Different parts of the brain decode the word by separating it into phonemes; identify the word as a whole; and address vocabulary, concept, and reason (Sousa 2011). A person comes to any text with prior experiences, and hopefully a purpose for reading. As people read, they relate the text to themselves and to other information, and they may integrate or apply what they read. Reading also depends on cognitive and social development; physical development is also needed to physically handle reading material and be in a position to sustain a reading experience.

In terms of reading stages, beginning readers focus on decoding and pronouncing words. When they connect a word with prior knowledge, they can comprehend the word. Reading fluency requires accurate and quick reading so that readers can focus on the meaning of the text. In addition, readers need to have a sufficient vocabulary to understand words in context. Mature readers are self-directed learners who interact with the text and context using a repertoire of strategies to understand and apply text in a self-reflective manner (Weaver 2002).

Many youth with ASDs also have language disorders, which can affect their reading competence. They may also have auditory problems, which affects how they hear words. Their brains have different activation patterns, with more action in the right hemisphere (the visual side) and less in the left (the language-oriented side). In addition, the posterior part of the brain, which deals with perceiving details, is more active in youth with ASDs. These different parts of the brain do not synchronize as well as brains of youth without ASDs, which can affect higher-level thinking and analysis (Just et al. 2004). In terms of processing textual information, youth with ASDs may have difficulty determining the main ideas, and they tend to have less self-awareness, which affects their reflective thinking. Because they often have narrow interests, youth with ASDs tend to have limited experiences and vocabulary. As noted before, youth with ASDs usually have physical development delays, so they may have difficulty physically sounding out words and handling a book; the reading environment may also distract them from reading. Likewise, their social skills tend to be behind those of their peers, so they have fewer social experiences and are not as motivated to share reading experiences.

A Word about Hyperlexia

Some children have a precocious ability to fluently read aloud a "grown-up" text, but without understanding what they have read. Hyperlexia is usually associated with advanced reading ability—and with ASDs. Children with hyperlexia have the ability to decode words and text at very advanced levels, usually at a very early age, but without being able to comprehend the meanings of the words they are decoding. They often have significant difficulty understanding and using verbal language, or they have a significant nonverbal learning disability. They also have difficulty in reciprocal interactions; they rarely start conversations, and they may resort to using echolalia. However, these children often have excellent visual and auditory memories, which they use to help them learn language. Indeed, some children with hyperlexia learn to speak solely through rote memory and much repetition. Some other symptoms of hyperlexia include a fixation on letters or words, ritualistic behavior, selective hearing, giftedness in some areas and notable deficiencies in others, awkward social skills, and difficulty with transitions. Hyperlexia is found as often in girls as in boys.

Two types of hyperlexia have been medically defined: language disorder and visual-spatial disorder. The former is more common; children with language disorder make more phonic errors and have difficulty with language pragmatics. They tend to have a lower verbal IQ and a higher performance IQ. Children with visual-spatial disorder make few phonic errors and have a higher verbal IQ and a lower nonverbal IQ. Typically, the visual and language parts of the brain are not integrated, which explains the disconnect between the visual nature of words and their meanings (Richman and Wood 2002).

Fortunately, children with hyperlexia can use their language skills to jump-start other aspects of reading and communication. For instance, they can associate gestured social cues with words to increase understanding. Likewise, they can examine picture books in terms of seeing examples of body language, thereby strengthening their ability to interpret bodily social messages. Story plots can teach them social skills, which may be a deficiency of youth with hyperlexia. Written communication, rather than spoken word, can be the main vehicle for communication. Whenever possible, reading guidance should build on the child's intent to communicate, because motivation can stretch the child's effort to learn reading skills.

READING SKILLS

Kimberly Henry (2010) has worked in depth on reading instruction for youth with ASDs, and she has made several suggestions for each aspect of reading development.

Phonic Awareness

Youth with ASDs usually have auditory processing issues, so it is difficult for them to distinguish sounds. Several techniques help children work with individual sounds:

- using a mirror to see how the mouth forms sounds
- comparing the motions with those of an adult
- playing word games
- generating rhymes
- softly beating time to poetry
- quietly singing
- using consonant-vowel-consonant words (e.g., *cat, dog*)
- focusing on words that are pronounced as they are spelled

Alphabet, alliterative (e.g., *Sheep on a Ship,* by Nancy Shaw and Margot Apple, Sandpiper, 1992), and rhyming books (e.g., *Moses Supposes His Toeses Are Roses,* by Nancy Patz, Harcourt Brace Jovanovich, 1983) provide great practice. The website of children's literature expert Nancy Keane offers several applicable lists (www.nancykeane.com).

Vocabulary

Youth with ASDs find naming objects the easiest type of vocabulary, and "what" questions are the simplest for them to answer. Some of the ways to expand the vocabulary of these youth include the following:

- teaching synonyms and antonyms
- matching words that go together, such as *swim* and *water*
- creating analogies, such as "Banana is to yellow as plum is to purple"
- building sets of contingent words, such as *beach, sand, ocean, waves, and boat*
- creating thematic word walls with picture cues
- matching pictures and words
- playing Pictionary
- playing Mad Libs to teach grammar and syntax
- writing down words used in daily life to build on social language
- watching closed-captioned television and movies
- creating picture books
- customizing augmentative and alternative communication, such as through a personal Picture Exchange Communication System.

It should be noted that youth with ASDs can become dependent on pictures, so their use needs to be faded out over time.

Comprehension

Youth with ASDs have difficulty making abstract connections, such as with predictions or inferences. They may have a limited sense of time, and so have difficulty conceptualizing the past and the future. They also often lack social skills to understand another person's point of view. Even when they do comprehend a text, because they tend not to use refined body language and to have a hard time using expressive language, it can be challenging to determine their level of understanding. Several techniques can aid these youth in comprehending texts:

- starting with concrete nonfiction reading
- relating the text and characters to the child

- making predictions based on the cover and inside images
- modeling think-aloud reading strategies
- retelling the story
- dramatizing the story
- drawing what is read
- explicitly teaching about feelings by referring to images
- building background knowledge
- distinguishing between fact and fiction
- using graphic organizers such as T-charts for comparisons and story trains for sequencing plot points

Jed Baker's 2001 book *Social Skills Picture Book* shows how to help youth with ASDs gain social skills while learning to read. Joseph Porter's 2011 book *Autism and Reading Comprehension* contains many ready-to-use lessons on CD for teachers.

Fluency

Youth with ASDs tend to read aloud with little expression. They recognize words in isolation but sometimes cannot understand them in context. Choral reading, repeating refrains, echoing text, and repeatedly listening to audiotapes all help these youth read more fluently. In addition, books with predictable text such as *The Little Red Hen* help them with prediction and rhythm. Adapted stories that explicitly focus on a reading skill can also be helpful (for examples, see the website Learn to Read, at www.starfall.com/n/level-a/learn-to-read/play.htm?f).

READING GUIDANCE

Building on good reading instructional practices, librarians can help youth with ASDs have positive reading experiences. Particularly because librarians see these youth across the curriculum, they have a big-picture perspective. Moreover, librarians can emphasize the visceral aspects of reading and promote reading as a pleasurable activity that can be done independently or as a social experience. As a start, librarians can create a positive reading environment by displaying attractive reading material, providing comfortable seating, and making quiet areas available.

STORY HOURS

Story hours are a mainstay program feature of youth-serving libraries. Story hours have several benefits for youth with ASDs: they offer
whole-language reading opportunities, they provide a low-risk social
activity, and they model voluntary reading enjoyment. Although story
hours can be conducted specifically for youth with ASDs, having a heterogeneous group enables youth to learn from one another more.

The conditions for successful story hours begin with the environment itself. It should be comfortable, accessible, and free of distractions. Story-hour carpet squares enable each child to have a unique
defined space, which is comforting for children with ASDs. These
squares should be set far enough apart so that children's bodies do not
touch one another's and so that if a child starts to rock or fidget, it will
not bother the group. There also needs to be some open space, as some
children may need to move around. The librarian should try to find out
whether any adults, such as a parent or aide, will accompany the child
so that adequate space can be provided for that person. It is also a good
idea to have a few fidget toys for children to hold as they listen. A pad-
ded, weighted belt or heavy pillow can also provide physical grounding.

Most story hours have a routine: an opening and closing activity, as
well as the story. These rituals help focus the audience and provide
happy predictability. Some openings work better than others; candles
can be problematic because of the flame and the odor, linking hands
and arms can be stressful, and loud noises can be irritating for youth
with ASDs. Gentle wind chimes and soft singing are more acceptable
options. A visual schedule of the story hour helps children make smooth
transitions. Story hours should also have predictable rules so that children know how to behave. A typical story hour can be videotaped for a
child to view at home and be prepared when attending the story hour
"for real." In general, story hours should be somewhat shorter than
usual for youth with ASDs.

Story hours need planning, especially to address the needs of youth
with ASDs. As much as possible, at least one story or activity should
match the child's interest. Therefore, getting to know children's preferences ahead of time helps in choosing resources and activities. A thematic
approach provides welcome continuity and predictability. Especially for

continuing story-hour programs, repeating a story or poem from the prior session is a positive way to engage children and reinforce memory.

Some basic practices can optimize story hours for youth with ASDs. First, speech can be difficult for children with ASDs. The librarian should speak clearly and project well. He or she may need to state and restate directions. When asking questions, the librarian should wait for feedback and consider alternative ways for children to participate, such as raising hands or making a thumbs-up sign. It's also OK if youngsters don't seem to respond; the important thing is to provide opportunities for participation.

Second, visuals are important. Big books enable all children to see well. The cover can be used as a prediction activity and as a way to introduce background information. Stories should relate to real life. Saying things such as "I wonder what happens next" while turning the page can teach prediction skills and engage children actively.

Story hours should be kept simple and multisensory. Children can quietly clap out rhythms or do vocal play. Props and puppets can extend the reading experience. Bubbles can add fun and acceptable spontaneity. If gestures are part of the activity, use large motor muscles rather than small finger movements.

D'Orazio (2007) has listed several good songs and big books that work well for story hours involving children with ASDs.

Behavior management also needs to be addressed in story hour. Probably the best seat for a child with an ASD is close to the front and off to one side. U-shaped seating works well, with everyone facing the front. Designating a story-hour buddy for children with ASDs is a good preventative measure. Minor incidents of misbehavior or unusual behavior can usually be ignored if it does not bother others. However, if a child's behavior poses a threat to him- or herself or to others, then immediate action is necessary. If the audience seems to be losing interest, it is probably time to change the activity or try a new approach. Often, youth with ASDs might not exhibit enthusiasm or even comprehension, but they may be listening and enjoying themselves, so it can be difficult to gauge the difference between introspection and boredom. Likewise, repetitive movement and sound can signal both stress and positive arousal. Whenever possible, librarians should get to know the child ahead of time, and talk with the child's support team to identify behavior cues. In any case, the librarian needs to convey acceptance of and respect for all children. Nevertheless, having a plan B (and a plan C) can help librarians maintain composure.

REFERENCES

Baker, J. *Social Skills Picture Book*. Arlington, TX: Future Horizons, 2001.

D'Orazio, A. "Small Steps, Big Results." *Children and Libraries* (2007): 21–23.

Henry, K. *How Do I Teach This Kid to Read?* Arlington, TX: Future Horizons, 2010.

Just, A., V. Cherkassky, T. Keller, and N. Minshew. "Cortical Activation and Synchronization during Sentence Comprehension in High-Functioning Autism: Evidence of Underconnectivity." *Brain* 127 (2004): 1811–21.

Notbohm, E., and V. Zysk. *1001 Great Ideas for Teaching and Raising Children with Autism or Asperger's*. 2nd ed. Arlington, TX: Future Horizons, 2010.

Porter, J. *Autism and Reading Comprehension: Ready-to-Use Lessons for Teachers*. Arlington, TX: Future Horizons, 2011.

Richman, L., and K. Wood. "Learning Disability Subtypes: Classification of High Functioning Hyperlexia." *Brain and Language* 82 (2002): 10–21.

Sousa, D. *How the Brain Learns*. Thousand Oaks, CA: Corwin Press, 2011.

Weaver, C. *Reading Process and Practice*. 3rd ed. Portsmouth, NH: Heinemann, 2002.

CHAPTER 7

The Social Role of the Library

LIBRARIES ARE MORE THAN RESOURCES; THEY ARE PLACES WHERE PEOple can get engaged with their heads and their minds. They are content-rich environments where people of all stripes can collectively exchange ideas and feelings. Libraries serve as an acceptable, safe place for youth with ASDs to pursue their own interests and interact with others in socially appropriate ways. Therefore, librarians should leverage the public role of the library to support the socialization of youth with ASDs. This chapter examines some of those issues and how to address them.

LIBRARIAN SOCIAL ENGAGEMENT

The library can be a safe and inviting atmosphere for youth with ASDs. As a public institution, the library can also serve as a way for these youth to build social skills, using resources and services alongside other people.

Probably the most effective way to engage youth with ASDs is to get to know each one on a personal basis. Librarians also need to get to know other adults who work with this population, including their families. To optimize socialization in school settings, school librarians should prepare the following groups to work with students with ASD: the child with an ASD him- or herself, library staff and aides (including students), other students, other teachers and school community members, the child's parents, and other parents. Public librarians are less likely to meet a child's service team, but they are more likely to work with families.

Starting with a personal introduction to the child even before relying on other information can provide a clean slate, as the librarian can get to know the child as a person without the extra baggage of labels. Meeting the child at eye level while maintaining respectful physical space sends a message of personal attention and respectful care. Usually, it is a good idea to meet the child alongside a family member or other service provider to have an introductory "bridge"; even if the child doesn't recognize that connection, the other adult will and can help the child remember the library and its staff. At this point, the librarian might find out what interests the child. The librarian can then use that information to briefly state the library staff's role as it relates to the child (e.g., "Oh, you like snakes? The library has good snake books. We can help you find a book about snakes. You can borrow the book and take it home.")

Of course, getting to know a child with ASD is not a one-shot or one-person effort, just as getting to know any individual is not. Because ASDs are diagnosed, librarians can get information about the child from the service team, other teachers, the family, and the child. Such information is very much appreciated, particularly as the librarian often sees the child in group settings. In schools, being able to see the IEP gives the librarian a heads-up on areas to monitor and helps the librarian collaborate more effectively with the classroom teacher to provide a valuable library experience. Some important pieces of information that can help interactions and behavior management follow. Ideally, having this list completed by the family or service team for each child with an ASD could greatly help the people who interact with the child and facilitate social situations. By knowing about the child's typical behavior and expectations as well as personal characteristics, the librarian can be better equipped to interact effectively with the child and can help the child interact successfully in the library environment, including:

- full name, and name preferred by the child
- trusted adults
- trusted peers
- favorite interests
- favorite books, television shows, films, and games
- strengths
- specific challenges
- sensory level (e.g., hypo, hyper, specific sensitivities)
- sound or noise tolerance (e.g., whether the child uses earplugs or earphones)
- typical activity level
- typical social behavior
- receptive and comprehension language development level
- communication level and preferred communication mode (e.g., availability of PECS)
- cognitive strengths and challenges
- stress triggers
- motivators and incentives (e.g., Cheerios, computer time, a toy), and whether a token system used
- typical stimulating actions and appropriate responses to them (e.g., ignore, redirect)
- effective behavior management strategies

With this information, the librarian can also inform the rest of the library staff and volunteers about effective ways to interact with the child and facilitate meeting his or her needs. Other library personnel might have made the child's acquaintance already, either in the library or in another setting, so they can also serve as conduits of information. Furthermore, since people have different personalities, it may be that the child has a favored library staffer who can be the main connection.

PEER SOCIAL ENGAGEMENT

Both public and school libraries serve youth, so youngsters with ASDs have opportunities to experience social situations with their peers. To optimize those experiences, librarians should provide the conditions for successful interaction by identifying and enlisting the help of supportive individuals and social groups.

One model is a buddy system, whereby a peer helps a child with ASDs in difficult social environments. For instance, break time in the library is often unstructured and can feel chaotic; having a library aide or other stable peer around to help direct youth with ASDs can relieve library staff from having to pay attention to that individual in the midst of working with competing demands. Usually, buddies take turns so that not one person has this job all the time; a dependable cadre of buddies can inform and support one another, serving as a social safety net for youth with ASDs.

Peer mentors can help youth with ASDs with academic, communication, and social skills. This strategy works well in the library for tasks such as using the library catalog and online resources, and it can be part of a library aide's work with all library users. Peers can also help youth with ASDs and others with information literacy skills, such as evaluating websites and taking notes. Although not done frequently, peers can also serve as personal reader's advisers if trained by the librarian. Peer mentors not only serve as "little librarians" but also hone their own library skills and teaching expertise.

It should be noted (again) that youth with ASDs can also serve as library aides and peer mentors, leveraging their own expertise to help younger or less able youth. For instance, a child with ASDs might glom on to an online reference tool or software program and spend hours learning its features. That child can then serve as the resident expert or go-to person for that resource. A "genius bar" can be a valuable service in the library, where a library aide or mentor can hang out at a computer service desk supplied with a couple of stations and joint viewing monitor, and provide help upon request.

A third social model is a circle of friends. These peers know one another and consider the youth with an ASD a friend as well. They help youth with ASDs broaden their social repertoire and accept new social events. For instance, they might all go to a baseball game or school play together. A circle of friends can support one another and contribute to social communication. Particularly since teens with ASDs are likely to have limited social opportunities and few out-of-school friends, a circle of friends can act as a significant social safety net, ensuring a dependable yet flexible social group. A circle of friends can also work with the youth's adult service team to plan kid-friendly interventions (Plimley, Bowen, and Morgan 2007). For the circle of friends to be successful, the child with an ASD should be able to choose the friends—at least some of them—and the friends should be able to opt out if they are asked to serve in this capacity. Otherwise, they may feel that they are being foisted onto the child. Sometimes, one or two peers can start the circle and then invite other friends as the need arises or as the level of acceptance increases.

Although a circle of friends is usually not under the librarian's control, it certainly is a group that should be called on by the librarian or at least made known to library staff. If the library sponsors a library aide or other type of cocurricular library club (e.g., book club, social media club, anime club, reviewers' group, storytellers, steering committee) that includes youth with ASDs, that group might serve as a natural, authentic circle of friends. In that respect, being a library aide should have a social dimension to strengthen group identity and foster cohesion. Therefore, librarians are encouraged to sponsor library-friendly groups that provide positive learning and social activities.

SOCIAL SKILLS DEVELOPMENT

As noted before, youth with ASDs are developmentally behind their peers in social skills. The reasons for such differences are many: sensory processing differences, difficulties in receptive or expressive language, body sense differences, and so on. These differences manifest in several ways to a greater or lesser degree (Moyes 2001):

- difficulties perceiving different perspectives
- difficulties imitating and doing pretend play
- little facial expression
- poor eye contact
- difficulties reading facial expressions and other body language
- difficulties practicing self-awareness (e.g., being obnoxious, personal hygiene)
- difficulties controlling emotions and anxiety

- difficulties sharing thoughts and feelings
- difficulties seeking and offering comfort
- difficulties handling praise or criticism

Librarians can work with families, the youth's service team, and other service providers to discern how to understand these youth socially and to help them improve their social skills. Not only will youth with ASDs become more socially competent and have a greater social network, they will learn more, since much of learning is socially constructed.

Building Social Skills at the Individual Level

Quill (1995) provides a useful step-by-step approach for generally addressing and improving social skills of youth with ASDs:

1. **Target the social situation.** Is anything causing a problem? What is difficult for the child to do? What might be the consequences of change?
2. **Gather data about the child.** What are the child's interests, abilities, impairments, and motivations? What factors affect the social situation and the child's reaction? From the child's point of view, what objects, people, and interactions affect the social situation?
3. **Share observations with the service team and the child.** Identify the triggers and social cues. Describe the situation objectively. Review the child's observations and "read" back the social situation (i.e., a social review). Identify alternative reactions or behaviors that would be more socially acceptable. State the benefits of acting according to social norms in terms of the child's perspective (e.g., "If you take turns, you are more likely to have a chance to do what you want to do."). Create social stories as a way to teach social skills.
4. **Identify and support new social skills.** Have the child self-identify his or her new response and social skill. Support new social skills using the Picture Exchange Communication System.

Step 3 mentions social stories, a term coined by Carol Gray in 1991 (Gray and Garand 1993). The concept of a social story is an individualized short story that helps a child understand and behave appropriately in social situations. Normally, such stories are highly prospective and structured. They describe the social situation in terms of social cues, noting the perspective of others and showing an appropriate behavior; they explain both actions and the motivations for those actions. They usually consist of short sentences and child-appropriate vocabulary, often including one step per page with an accompanying image. Although *social story* is a trademarked term, the underlying idea of showing a child a step-by-step explanation of a social situation, and how to react in such a situation, is a standard practice. The story approach provides psychological distance that can make the message easier to understand. Social stories can be purchased, but they might need to be individualized to fit the child's situation and personal behaviors.

Play Skills

Play helps youth connect with an activity and with others, and it provides an enjoyable structure in which to practice skills. It can lift a person's spirits, and it fosters flexibility and creativity. Play skills are developmental, as noted before. Children learn to link sensory movement and functional play (e.g., moving a toy car), play functions concretely (e.g., making zoom noises when playing with a toy car), and then play thematically or symbolically (e.g., having a toy-car race).

In terms of social development, play helps youth with ASDs become aware that other people have different perspectives, and it motivates youth with ASDs to figure out what other people think and adjust their own behavior accordingly. Play teaches cooperation, give-and-take, and ways to deal with loss. Fortunately, most youth with ASDs like rules, so having structure helps them play appropriately. Youth with ASDs have to explicitly learn to value typical social rewards, and they may need to be convinced that play will benefit them. Highly competitive play should probably be avoided, although self-competition can be an acceptable way for youth with ASDs to self-improve. For an interesting set of videos to build social skills, see the website Different Roads to Learning (www.difflearn.com/category/video_modeling).

Play skills occur in the library, particularly for elementary grade children as they act out a story or do other post-story activities. In upper grades, play is part of role-playing and the use of games to reinforce literacy skills. Librarians can even use books to promote play skills; children can evaluate a character to see what play skills he or she exhibits; the Frances (by Russell Hoban, HarperCollins) and Berenstain Bears (by Stan and Jan Berenstain, Random House) stories, as well as sports books, are good for this activity. Playing a game about characters is a way to build play skills while improving literacy competence.

Sharing

Here are several ways to help children share:

- Split an item, such as food.
- Split the amount of time that one can use an item (take turns); use a timer to ensure equity.
- Model good sharing behavior.
- Let each child have one thing that he or she does not have to share.
- Remand sharing privileges if the child treats the item badly.
- Read and discuss stories about sharing (see Utah's Logan Library's list of children's books at http://library.loganutah .org/books/children/sharing.cfm).

Body Language

Youth with ASDs have difficulties understanding and using facial expressions and other body language. It should be noted that most children have difficulty reading some facial expressions, particularly fear, so in that respect, youth with ASDs should not be singled out. Nevertheless, youth with ASDs have specific challenges; they can have a hard time controlling and expressing emotions in general, maintaining eye contact (which impedes facial analysis), controlling body movements, and coordinating their bodies to perform sequences of action.

Some picture books, especially those with clear photographs, can help youth identity and distinguish facial expressions; specific elements need to be pointed out and compared with other expression for all children to be able to understand and replicate expressions. Simple images, such as emoticons, highlight these specific expressive elements, such as raised eyebrows or frowns, but they are abstractions that may be difficult for youth with ASDs to associate with real people. Complex images, such as realistic portraits, contain extraneous details that youth might focus on in lieu of specific expressive elements. Some youth find cartoon television programs (e.g., *Thomas the Tank Engine, Transporters,* and anime) to be good sources of information because the images are stylized but usually easier to interpret than realistic human faces. Software programs such as the interactive set of games called Let's Face It! enable users to mimic facial expressions to advance in the play (Tanaka et al. 2010).

For body language, analyzing emotional television shows and films is probably the easiest way to understand body language. Especially if good clips can be chosen and the medium can be paused, librarians and other service providers can help youth with ASDs deconstruct the critical features that define an emotion through body position and movement. Animated films, such as Disney movies, are easier to decipher than live-action ones. Paired with emotional stories, librarians can have youth mimic body gestures and movements as a group. Even though the movement will be a bit stereotyped, it gives a general idea about the connection between body and emotion. Sometimes, for nonverbal youth with ASDs, mirroring their body language, even though it may seem inarticulate, is a way to communicate with them and bridge their social gap. If for no other reason than that the other person is paying attention to the child and trying to relate to him or her, such proactive gestures can viscerally communicate the use of the body to express wants and needs.

THE SOCIAL SIDE OF EMOTIONS

Sharing emotions is an important part of socialization. Dr. John Gottman (2004) asserted that children who understand and handle their emotions form stronger friendships, calm themselves down and bounce back more quickly, have fewer negative emotions, succeed more in school, and stay healthier.

As with young neurotypical children, pretend play can be a way for children with ASDs to express emotions in a safe, nonverbal way. For instance, a child can pretend that she is a hurt animal, or that he was given a very special treat. Such role-play provides an emotional distance so that they child does not have to self-disclose emotions but can still practice how to express emotions in socially acceptable ways.

Librarians can share books about emotions, explicitly directing children to the images and words associated with different emotions, as well as showing how different ways to react emotionally can be more or less effective socially. Children can act out the story afterward to experience viscerally the role of emotions in social situations. LeRoy Collins Leon County (Florida) Public Library System has created a good starting list of picture books about emotions arranged categorically (www.leoncounty fl.gov/library/youth-child/images/Emotions-by-category.pdf).

Low- and nonverbal youth with ASDs might use a Picture Exchange Communication System (PECS) or assistive technology such as a speaking board to express emotions using language. The Smurks app displays hundreds of emoticons that the user can tweak.

When youth with ASDs do act out, such as having a temper tantrum, they first need to be calmed down. Once they can pay attention, the other person, such as a librarian, can help them understand the consequences of their actions. For instance, if a middle schooler hits an adult, the adult can respond naturally by saying, "Ouch, you hurt me," and showing pain. The youth can usually identify the emotion associated with pain. Then the adult can ask questions such as "Why am I sad?" to help the child figure out the relationship between hitting and the physical and emotional pain of being hit. At that point, the adult can say, "When you are angry, don't hit me. Tell me you are mad." Once the youth understands the socially acceptable use of words to express emotion, then the adult can work with the youth to figure out the basis for hitting and problem solve how to meet the obvious need of that youth. The social cue "Use your words" may be enough reinforcement in the future when the youth's emotions are about to boil over (Robinson 2011).

REFERENCES

Gottman, J. *What Am I Feeling?* Alameda, CA: Parenting Press, 2004.

Gray, C., and J. Garand. "Social Stories: Improving Responses of Students with Autism with Accurate Social Information." *Focus on Autistic Behavior* 8 (1993): 1–10.

Moyes, R. *Incorporating Social Goals in the Classroom.* London: Jessica Kingsley Publishers, 2001.

Plimley, L., M. Bowen, and H. Morgan. *Autistic Spectrum Disorders in the Early Years*. London: Paul Chapman, 2007.

Quill, K. *Teaching Children with Autism*. New York: Delmar, 1995.

Robinson, R. *Autism Solutions*. Don Mills, ON: Harlequin, 2011.

Tanaka, J., J. Wolf, C. Klaiman, K. Koenig, J. Cockburn, L. Herlihy, C. Brown, S. Stahl, M. Kaiser, and R. Schultz. "Using Computerized Games to Teach Face Recognition Skills to Children with Autism Spectrum Disorder: The Let's Face It! Program." *Journal of Child Psychology and Psychiatry* 51 (2010): 944–52.

Behavior Management

O NE OF THE PRECONDITIONS FOR LEARNING IS A SAFE AND functional environment, which includes monitoring and managing the people within that environment. Much of the literature about youth with ASDs centers on behavior management, which is not surprising, as criteria for diagnosis of ASDs include impairments of communication and social interaction.

Youth with ASDs may behave inappropriately regularly or situationally. In the former case, the reason is usually lack of social or cognitive skill; the person usually is not aware that he or she is behaving inappropriately and sees no reason for change. In the latter case, dysfunctional behavior can occur because of health issues (e.g., asthma, diabetes, sleep problems, gastrointestinal issues) or trigger events such as stress, feeling overwhelmed, fear or anxiety, anger, frustration, loss of control, discomfort, pain, exhaustion, communication limitations, emotional negative associations, and psychosis. Stereotypical behaviors such as hand flapping or rocking can usually be ignored, or the youth can be redirected with minimal attention. However, self-injurious behavior such as aggression and destruction need to be stopped for the safety of everyone involved. In addition, some youth with ASDs are hypersensitive and tend to overreact, whereas other youth with ASDs are hyposensitive and may seem passive or disengaged. Responses to these factors can be manifest in several ways.

Dozens of behavior management models exist, each of which aims to facilitate the learning of self-regulation techniques as well as social and communication skills. The National Autism Center's 2009 National Standards Project rated major treatments, including emerging and ineffective ones. According to Myers and Johnson (2007), most effective treatment programs believe in early, intensive interventions that deeply involve the family. The treatments are individualized, structured and systematic, and implemented in a predictable environment. They use a functional approach to reduce challenging behaviors, finding out why a child behaves in a certain way and then replacing that dysfunctional behavior with a more positive and effective one.

Nevertheless, there is no current law that requires that any classroom teacher other than an education specialist (i.e., special education teacher) needs to know any methodologies for working specifically with youth with ASDs. Even many education specialists do not receive in-depth training about ASDs. Nor does the No Child Left Behind Act (Pub. L. No. 107-110) explicitly address the rights of children with special needs. Given that at least 1 percent of school-age children are diagnosed with ASDs, it seems logical that training in ASDs should be mandatory for K–12 teachers.

As a corollary, librarians should know some of the behavior management skills that apply to youth with ASDs so they can help them have more positive library experiences.

ASSESSMENT

Regardless of the program, the first step is assessment. In assessment, the expert collects and interprets data about the youth to diagnose the situation and design appropriate interventions. In terms of behavior management, most likely a psychologist will observe the youth's behavior and determine his or her social-emotional development stage.

The assessor examines how the youth interacts in meaningful context with different people, identifies his or her communication strengths, and gets data about what helps and impedes appropriate behavior. When assessing teens, the expert analyzes how the person communicates with different types of people, from family to community members, looking at the results and key supports.

When focusing on problem behaviors, the expert tries to identify the conditions that triggered or preceded the inappropriate behavior and the reinforcing consequences. The behavior itself is a form of communication, be it conscious or unconscious, and is usually done for a purpose. For instance, a teen may act out because he doesn't want to do a challenging task or work with a group. Another child might repeated fall out of her chair. The expert then chooses (or helps the youth choose) a more effective communication method and teaches the youth to use it. In the former example, the teen learns to verbalize his frustration to the librarian; in the latter example, the librarian could fit a chair with well-defined "bumper" edges, which would help the child situate herself physically.

APPLIED BEHAVIORAL ANALYSIS

Probably the most established behavioral management method is applied behavioral analysis (ABA). Hall (2009) has explained each word in the phrase:

> **Applied:** principles that can be applied in all kinds of settings that have social significance to the person with ASDs
>
> **Behavioral:** observable, measurable actions that are the focus of the intervention
>
> **Analysis:** data collection, measurement, and assessment used to determine an intervention's effectiveness

Overall, ABA applies research-based behavioral principles in interventions to improve specific behaviors and to determine the effectiveness of those interventions. The theoretical grounding of ABA is positivism (i.e., observable and objective approach) and behaviorism (i.e., relationship between stimulus and response). It uses very specific strategies and should be conducted under the supervision of a board-certified professional. Nevertheless, librarians who work with youth with ASDs will find it useful to understand ABA's key concepts, as it can be used to support social, academic, and independent functioning skills.

Reinforcement is a central feature of ABA. Positive reinforcement is used to increase desired behaviors, and negative reinforcement occurs when a behavior reduces or delays a stimulus. For instance, a child learns to say hello when introduced to a person but not indiscriminately throughout the day (Hall 2009). Some strategies for discrimination training include matching-to-sample procedures, stimulus generalization, and errorless learning. The schedule of reinforcement is almost always important because at the beginning, reinforcement is given each time a desired behavior occurs, to transition the child from partial performance to full competence. Once the target behavior is established, intermittent reinforcement works more effectively to sustain the behavior. In any case, the supervisor has to determine what kinds of reinforcers work most effectively for the child; usually, both contrived (e.g., sticker, cracker, stamp) and natural (e.g., computer time, choice of activity) rewards are used. Positive attention such as conversing or joining in an activity can also serve as a reinforcer. Some of the other social supports include social integration, reassurance of reliable alliances, social buddies, and opportunities for nurturance.

A critical aspect of ABA is operationalizing target behaviors. Key behaviors are identified first in light of the youth's daily life, such as learning how to take turns. The educator identifies all the skills and how they need to be sequenced to perform a complex behavior. The youth is then assessed in terms of his or her ability to do the task, with the intent of identifying the discrepancies between the current and the target behavior. At that point, the skills are taught in the setting that most approximates the ultimate task (e.g., learning how to wash hands at a sink).

Leach (2010) listed a rich repertoire of other teaching strategies:

- arranging the environment for optimum behavior
- following the youth
- contingent imitation: imitating the youth's behavior to establish interaction

- modeling to help the person imitate the behavior, such as making requests
- video modeling
- peer-mediated intervention
- social stories
- direct instruction
- teaching self-monitoring
- shaping: reinforcing increasingly close approximation of a desired behavior
- behavior momentum: increasing motivation when a challenging task is required

PIVOTAL RESPONSE TREATMENT

Pivotal response treatment (PRT) is a comprehensive service-delivery model that uses both a developmental approach and applied behavior analysis procedures (Koegel and Koegel 2006). Based on ABA, it aims to provide opportunities for learning within the context of the child's natural environment. Pivotal response treatment tries to identify key behaviors that can affect several functional areas and facilitate generalized improvement.

Pivotal response treatment is most impactful as an intensive early intervention, conducted at least twenty hours per week in a natural setting, such as the home. The family plays a key role in designing and delivering the interventions. Pivotal response treatment works on the basis of motivating the child to engage in social-communicative interaction. The social initiation to joint attention and shared pleasure can lead to behavior self-regulation.

Because PRT uses a developmental approach, different strategies are appropriate at different ages. In early childhood, natural language consequences are used, such as placing a desirable item in view but out of reach or providing part of a desired item; educators respond to the child's interests and strengths (which are usually nonverbal) and provide the desired item contingent on the child's response. In preschool, social skills are expanded to include new adults and peers, and the child learns school-readiness skills such as letters and colors. Elementary children learn how to work in small groups, and they are given praise rather than concrete rewards for work well done. Middle and high school youth learn lifelong social activities, such as camping. At each level, educators refine goals and their own role, and they consider the youth's peers to be resources.

As with most behavior modification systems, PRT screens for communication and socialization, looking for predictive behaviors such as lack of joint attention, communication delays, lack of pretend play, and repetitive or restrictive interests. Based on the assessment, an intervention is designed to be embedded into the child's daily program. Typically, the educator marks when a task is completed and reinforces repeated positive behaviors; over time, the child learns to self-monitor his or her behavior. In PRT, the educator adjusts tasks in response to the child's personal situation (e.g., stressed because of a disruption in the day's routine) and preemptively tries to prepare the child for changes ahead of time. Basically, the aim of PRT is to provide a safe learning environment so youth can take positive intellectual and social risks with guidance to get them past fears. Some of the social supports include social integration, reassurance of worth, reliable alliances, social buddies, and opportunities for nurturance.

SOCIAL COMMUNICATION, EMOTIONAL REGULATION, AND TRANSACTIONAL SUPPORT

The tenets of social communication, emotional regulation, and transactional support (SCERTS) address core developmental challenges and assert that developmental domains are interdependent (Prizant et al. 2006). The SCERTS model focuses on functional use of language and communication in the context of natural environments. The child's emotional regulation and its effect on interaction and learning are analyzed, and arousal states are constantly monitored. The environment is arranged, and activities are designed to help motivate the child to begin social communication, which leads to spontaneous functional communication. The SCERTS model helps youth grow socially and emotionally to develop a sense of self-pride, independence, a sense of others, flexibility, resilience, cooperation, social membership, and friendship.

Transactional support promotes active in-depth participation, peer interaction, and positive relationships with adults. Strategies include interpersonal support, learning support, and support to families and their teams. To this end, SCERTS provides purposeful learning experiences with peers, who provide appropriate language and social models, which helps youth with ASDs build meaningful peer relationships. Activities tend to be goal oriented, thematic, and cooperative. Sequenced skills are embedded in each activity, and transactional support is given for social communication and emotional regulation as youth practice skills. Concepts are introduced gradually and modeled. The teacher provides consistency and predictability, and gives clear prompts and signals. Variety is added to activities to help learners generalize skills to new settings and to create communication opportunities. Wetherby and colleagues (2005) noted SCERTS practices that apply well to library settings:

- Follow the youth's focus of attention, and respond to his or her intended goals.
- Expand on a child's play and communication efforts.
- Encourage imitation when the child is focused.
- Get down physically to the child's level when communicating.
- Adjust language input quality to the youth's development and arousal level.
- Alternate between active and sedentary experiences.
- Structure activity to facilitate participation, such as taking turns.
- Foster initiation by letting the youth start and stop the activity.
- Respect independence by letting the youth take a break to move about as appropriate.
- Give the youth time to solve problems independently and complete tasks.

SAMPLE PROGRAMS FOR PRESCHOOLERS

The Treatment and Education of Autistic and Related Communication Handicapped Children (TEACCH) program focuses on adapting the child's physical environment and providing visual cues to help youth act independently (O'Brien and Daggett 2006). For instance, areas are defined, distractions are minimized, and physical transitions are simplified. The youth is assessed using the Psycho Educational Profile (PEP) to design an individualized program; the educator serves as a cross-cultural "interpreter," helping youth become more comfortable in their social world. As with other treatments, TEACCH builds on the child's strengths to teach new skills in a visually structured manner: creating work-activity systems that delineate parameters of time and task sequence. However, unlike some other treatments, TEACCH takes a more holistic approach and accepts the youth's deficits. The TEACCH program believes in a culture of autism, which has characteristic patterns of understanding the world and communicating. In this culture, behaviors have a limited central coherence in which concrete thinking is more common than abstraction, and generalizations from one setting to another are difficult. Sensory and perceptual differences, strong interests and impulses, excessive anxiety, and disorganization mark this culture.

Learning Experiences: An Alternative Program (LEAP) promotes interactions between youth with ASDs and their peers, with a focus on peer-mediated interventions. It emphasizes consistency across school and home, and LEAP is usually implemented as a developmentally integrated preschool that builds on parent-teacher collaboration (Hall 2009).

The program Developmental, Individual-Difference, Relationship-Based Floor Time (DIR/Floor Time) builds on understanding the child's sensory differences and following the child's lead (Greenspan and Wieder 2009). The teacher helps the child master core developmental stages:

1. **Regulation and interest in the world:** feeling calm, attending to surroundings, sharing attention
2. **Engagement and relation:** developing bonds with preferred caregivers, distinguishing inanimate objects from people
3. **Two-way intentional communication:** simple interaction, smiles, and anticipatory play
4. **Social problem solving:** using gestures and prelanguage to indicate needs and emotions, asking for help

5. **Symbolic plan:** using words, pictures, and symbols to communicate an intent or idea
6. **Bridging ideas**

The Relationship Development Intervention (RDI) deals with social-emotional relationships, focusing on remediation of brain-based deficits. The goal is to help youth enter uncertain situations with motivation and self-confidence. The main approach to reaching this goal is through parent-child relationships (Gutstein 2004). Communication is broadly defined in RDI, heightening shared experiences through nonverbal and other means of amplification.

The Early Start Denver Model is another parent-centric model. It uses social games to ensure that interactions are pleasurable. Discrete trial training is also incorporated in sensory social routines. This model is usually implemented as part of an intensive structured program that includes social interaction, communication, play skills, motor skills, cognitive skills, and personal independence (Rogers and Dawson 2009).

DEALING WITH MELTDOWNS

Some general advice can help prevent a potentially upsetting situation for children with ASDs:

1. Get to know the youth personally.
2. Modify expectations.
3. Modify the environment, and structure the environment for success.
4. Modify sensory input.
5. Look for positive outlets for unusual behavior.

Sometimes one can ignore a behavior as a way to help extinguish it. If minimal physically inappropriate behavior occurs, a brief restraint or inclusionary time-out (e.g., putting one's head on the desk) suffices. Only when the behavior is intrusive is a physical intervention needed.

Nevertheless, behaviors can get out of hand. Here are some symptoms of overstimulation that can lead to meltdowns (Notbohm and Zysk 2010):

- loss of balance or orientation
- skin flushes or paleness, or profuse sweating
- change in heart rate
- hysteria or crying
- stomachache, cramps, or nausea
- echolalia and self-calming behaviors, including "stimming"
- aggression or anger, or active refusal

Some trigger events can be cut short through specific interventions (Thompson 2008). For example, when obsessive-compulsive symptoms occur, provide an alternative captivating activity. Compulsive rituals should be prevented by varying choices of activities or materials.

To address social anxiety, provide the youth with an escape strategy, and teach communication skills to request leaving the situation. It is also a good idea to help desensitize youth by exposing them to partial aspects of the thing they fear.

Difficult tasks can be simplified or reduced to make them easier to complete. Tasks might be done in parts or accomplished as a group project.

A meltdown is usually signaled by anger or aggression, which leads to distress and remorse. Overall, it usually lasts fewer than ten minutes. When a meltdown occurs, several general steps can mitigate the problem behavior (Whitaker 2001):

1. Stay in emotional control. Respond consistently.
2. Make sure the environment is safe. Remove others if needed, and call for help if needed. Remove the trigger event if possible.
3. Respond to the behavior as a communication effort.
4. Get the youth's attention, and give a short verbal, concrete directive in a neutral tone. If the youth doesn't react, use a nonverbal prompt.
5. Make sure the youth becomes calm. Give the person space, and restore normalcy. Calmly restate rules and any requests, and talk the situation through.
6. Analyze the situation: the setting (place, people, and activity), the trigger event and sequence, the responding behavior, the

function of the behavior, and the consequences (Zarkowska and Clements 1994).

SAMPLE BEHAVIOR MANAGEMENT TECHNIQUES

As is the case with everyone, youth with ASDs run into problems as they try to deal with their environment. However, some approaches do not work well with youth with ASDs, such as peer pressure or verbal praise. The following proven techniques can be used specifically to help youth with ASDs behave appropriately in the library. In each case, the intervention should be closely monitored and assessed to determine its effectiveness, and modified as needed.

Odom and colleagues (2010) developed a useful comparative list of evidence-based interventions for youth with ASDs. Behavior-based practices of interest to librarians included discrete trial training, peer-mediated interventions, the Picture Exchange Communication System, pivotal response treatment, positive behavioral support strategies, reinforcement, self-management, social narratives, and video modeling. Several specific strategies are clustered under positive behavioral support strategies:

- functional behavior assessment, which determines the underlying function or purpose of an inappropriate behavior so that an effective intervention can be designed
- functional communication training, which replaces inappropriate behavior with appropriate communicative behaviors—in tandem with functional behavior assessment
- differential reinforcement, which rewards desired behaviors that are incompatible with inappropriate behaviors
- stimulus control and environmental modification
- response interruption and/or redirection
- extinction

Social narratives describe a social situation in terms of relevant cues, such as a binder of photos that show appropriate behavior sequentially for a specific situation. Video reenactments can also serve to show how to act in certain circumstances. A social story can give another person's perspective about a situation, which can help the youth think beyond his or her own universe of meaning. Librarians can create social stories about library procedures and keep them handy for new users or those who don't know how to act appropriately. These stories can also be borrowed to practice behaviors at home. When the youth knows how to perform appropriately but doesn't follow through, the librarian can perhaps identify at what point the behavior diverges and then work with the youth and support team to figure out an alternative. For instance, a youth might become aggressive in the library's checkout line because he or she is stressed about the end-of-class bell ringing. Perhaps the child can have a checkout buddy, go to the head of the line, or leave the item at the circulation desk to check out later.

A power card strategy is a variation of social stories (Myles, Trautman, and Schelvan 2006). Building on the youth's special interests, power cards are visual aids that reinforce skills. In three to five steps, a brief script explains what to do in a specific situation. Each step is shown on a separate card (the size of a credit card or index card), which the youth carries as a reminder. Power cards can be made into game-card formats and played as a game such as authors or a sequence game.

Self-management interventions for social communication represent a high-level solution for youth with ASDs. A trained expert usually teaches this approach, but the librarian can be informed of this intervention and can help reinforce it when the occasion arises in the library. Here are the steps for implementing this strategy, with library applications indicated in italic:

1. **Get ready.** Identify and analyze the current misbehavior. Choose a reinforcing reward, and select an initial goal. *Jim bangs the computer keyboard when frustrated. Jim likes to listen to music, so he gets to use a headphone and listen to a predetermined favorite song if he doesn't bang the computer for ten minutes.*

2. **Teach how to self-manage.** Gather the resources, identify the current and desired behaviors, record each relevant behavior, and reward self-management efforts. *Jim has a watch. The librarian gives him an index card and pencil to mark every time he wants*

to bang the computer. Jim is prompted to write down the current time when he receives the card. Every time Jim actually bangs the computer, he crosses his "want to bang" mark. Each computer has a "help stand" to put on top of the monitor to signal that assistance is requested. Jim signals for help and marks his card with an H whenever he uses the help stand. The librarian goes to Jim whenever the signal is up and marks the card with the current time, circling the H. After each ten-minute interval, the librarian goes to Jim, writes down the time, and draws a line after the marks on the card. If Jim has marked his card but not banged on the computer, the librarian lends him earbuds to listen to a song.

3. **Create independence.** Increase the time frame for self-managing the behavior, reduce reliance on prompts, increase the number of times needed to get the reward, and decrease the presence of the monitoring person. *The time frame is lengthened. Jim gets to listen to the music only after his task is done.*

Providing choices can sidestep possible behavior triggers. By giving youth with ASDs opportunities to control their environment or how they respond to it, librarians can lower restrictions and teach valuable skills. Choices can occur in terms of resources, interaction, and production. For instance, youth might choose the version of a book (e.g., audio, e-book, abridged print) or select one of several books on the same topic. Youth might choose the type of technology used to represent a concept (e.g., video, simulation), organize thoughts (e.g., organization application, spreadsheet), or communicate ideas (e.g., authoring tool, blog). Likewise, youth might choose how to demonstrate competence: drawing a picture, creating a photo journal, or conducting an experiment. It should be realized that the task of making choices itself can be difficult for youth with ASDs; librarians should start by offering just two choices, such as between two websites.

Sometimes a child continues to act inappropriately. By keeping track of a youth's dysfunctional behavior, the librarian can help the support team diagnose the root cause and find a working solution. A behavior chart lists before-and-after behavior and notes the reason for the inappropriate behavior. The time and place of the behavior is also noted. Here are some possible actions:

Before: The youth is told to do something, a change in activity occurs, the youth is moved, the youth is interrupted, the youth is told no.

Problem behavior: specific stereotypical action, specific self-injurious action, specific other-directed action

After (action): The librarian pays attention to the youth, the youth is given something, the youth withdraws his or her request, the youth loses a turn, the youth is removed from the area, the youth is ignored, the youth is punished.

Possible reason for behavior: to avoid doing something, to avoid someone or some place, transition issue, to obtain something, to get attention

Table 8.1 shows a simple behavior chart that can be used to record a child's behavior before and during an inappropriate action, the intervention used, and the rationale for the problem behavior. Recording such data can help the service providers evaluate the child's behavior over time and determine which interventions are effective.

Figure 8.1 **BEHAVIOR CHART**

	Jan. 15, 10:03 a.m.	Jan. 22, 10:22 a.m.	Jan. 29, 10:12 a.m.
BEFORE	Class bell rings	Start of drawing activity	Story ends
PROBLEM BEHAVIOR	Runs around the room	Tosses crayons and rips paper	Continues to repeat story's refrain
INTERVENTION	Stops child	Takes away supplies	Distracts child
REASON	Trouble settling down (transition)	Pushes too hard on paper (frustration?)	Doesn't want story to end (transition)

A WORD ABOUT RESPONSE TO INTERVENTION

As an alternative way to identify low-achieving students, response to intervention (RTI) can be used to address behaviors of youth with ASDs. The RTI model is a problem-solving model that attempts to prevent academic failure through early, research-based intervention and frequent monitoring. In RTI, learners who do not perform well are screened, and the basis for their low achievement is explored. Ideally, the educator finds a common reason and designs a targeted intervention as a way to remediate the group. Their progress is then monitored. For the subset of learners who do not respond to the intervention, a more specific and intensive intervention is developed and implemented. The remaining few learners who do not respond to this second tier of interventions are then referred to education specialists. This tiered service delivery enables all learners to receive core instruction and differentiation as applicable.

Response to intervention can be applied to youth with ASDs with challenging behaviors. The many tools to assess youth with ASDs could be applied to assessing the behaviors of all types of youth. Because other youth can also get frustrated or stressed, they could be grouped together to learn specific coping skills. If the dysfunctional behavior is due to some missing skill, other students along with youth having ASDs can learn this skill together. In the process, youth with ASDs can learn important social skills.

Librarians can support RTI efforts in several ways: locating appropriate resources; conducting research about proven interventions; and sharing ways that technology can be incorporated to help youth learn and demonstrate competence, such as concept maps, creative storyboarding, digital booktalks, online book reviews, mobile apps, the use of avatars, and wikis (Vanderbroek 2010). School librarians can also serve as remediators, taking one group of at-risk learners and working with them on specific interventions, such as extracting meaning from text, improving listening skills, and gaining reading fluency. Librarians can be particularly useful as instructional partners as they help design and deliver technology-enhanced interventions.

REFERENCES

Greenspan, S., and S. Wieder. *Engaging Autism: Using the Floortime Approach to Help Children Relate, Communicate, and Think.* Cambridge, MA: Da Capo, 2009.

Gutstein, S. *Going to the Heart of Autism.* Houston, TX: Connections Center, 2004.

Hall, L. *Autism Spectrum Disorders.* Upper Saddle River, NJ: Merrill, 2009.

Koegel, R., and L. Koegel. *Pivotal Response Treatments for Autism.* Baltimore: Paul H. Brookes, 2006.

Leach, D. *Bringing ABA into Your Inclusive Classroom.* Baltimore: Paul H. Brookes, 2010.

Myers S., and C. Johnson. "Management of Children with Autism Spectrum Disorders." *Pediatrics* 120 (2007): 1162–82.

Myles, B., M. Trautman, and R. Schelvan. *The Hidden Curriculum: Practical Solutions for Understanding Unstated Rules in Social Situations.* Shawnee Mission, KS: Autism Asperger Publishing, 2006.

National Autism Center. *National Standards Project: Findings and Conclusions.* Randolph, MA: National Autism Center, 2009.

Notbohm, E., and V. Zysk. *1001 Great Ideas for Teaching and Raising Children with Autism or Asperger's.* 2nd ed. Arlington, TX: Future Horizons, 2010.

O'Brien, M., and J. Daggett. *Beyond the Autism Diagnosis.* Baltimore: Paul H. Brookes, 2006.

Odom, S., L. Collet-Klingenberg, S. Rogers, and D. Hatton. "Evidence-Based Practices in Interventions for Children and Youth with Autism Spectrum Disorders." *Preventing School Failure* 54 (2010): 275–82.

Prizant, B., A. Wetherby, E. Rubin, A. Laurent, and P. Rydell. *The SCERTS Model.* Baltimore: Paul H. Brookes, 2006.

Rogers, S., and G. Dawson. *Early Start Denver Model for Young Children with Autism.* New York: Guilford Press, 2009.

Thompson, T. *Freedom from Meltdowns.* Baltimore: Paul H. Brookes, 2008.

Vanderbroek, A. "RTI: The Librarian's Fairy Tale?" *Library Media Connection* (2010): 48–50.

Wetherby, A., E. Rubin, A. Laurent, P. Rydell, and B. Prizant. *The SCERTS Model: A Comprehensive Educational Approach for Children with Autism Spectrum Disorders.* Baltimore: Paul H. Brookes, 2005.

Whitaker, P. *Challenging Behavior and Autism.* London: NAS, 2001.

Zarkowska, E., and J. Clements. *Problem Behaviour and People with Severe Learning Disabilities: The STAR Approach.* London: Nelson Thornes, 1994.

CHAPTER 9

Training

LIBRARY STAFF AND THE COMMUNITY AT LARGE NEED TRAINING to understand the nature of youth with ASDs and to suggest effective ways to serve this population. Although the basic facts about ASDs cross those audiences, the role that each stakeholder plays may differ. Therefore, each target group needs to explore different content and be approached in different ways.

OVERVIEW OF ASD TRAINING

The number of youth identified with ASDs has steadily increased. Especially since students with special needs are encouraged to be mainstreamed in heterogeneous classes, more educators need to be trained to ensure that these students have equitable educational experiences. Therefore, as an example of meeting that need, the Commission on Teacher Credentialing (2009) added a special authorization for ASDs. Teachers need to be able to identify the characteristics of students with ASDs and know this population's core challenges, including language and communication, neurology and cognition, behavior and social skills. Teachers need to be able to assess students to design and deliver instruction, using visual and positive behavior supports. Teachers also need to be able to collaborate with other service providers.

These competencies offer a useful baseline for training for librarians and community members, adjusting for different depths of knowledge and application. For instance, public librarians and paraprofessional library staff usually do just-in-time individual instruction rather than formal class instruction, as might school librarians conduct occasionally. Likewise, student library aides would learn age-appropriate information and would act under the supervision of adults.

Librarians might also provide training about ASDs to their clientele as part of their mission. In some systems, libraries have developed initiatives focused on ASDs and have included training as part of their charge. In general, ASD experts conduct training, although ASD-knowledgeable librarians can certainly team teach. State governments usually have an agency that is in charge of ASD services and can suggest groups or individuals to provide training. Some state universities have centers for ASD research or ASD training programs and can suggest speakers. Library associations might consider developing state databases of material and training resources. For instance, New York State has an initiative for adults and children on the autism spectrum, which includes a section on libraries (www.nyacts.com). It should be noted that experts are not necessarily effective trainers, so librarians should check with their counterparts to find out how well existing ASD trainings succeed. Positive Environments, Network of Trainers has good tips on developing effective trainings about special needs, including ASDs (www.pent.ca.gov/trn/training.html).

TRAINING FOR EDUCATORS

Both youth-serving public and school librarians deal with educators as they provide resources and services to youth with ASDs. By offering professional development opportunities for educators, particularly mainstream classroom teachers, librarians hold out a hand to collaborate in support of youth with ASDs. They also provide an opportunity for educators to realize the expertise that librarians have, as well as the kinds of resources that are relevant to youth with ASDs and their families and service providers. Even if librarians merely host such trainings, they are proactively showing interest in, and care for, both youth with ASDs and their service providers. The trainings are also great opportunities for librarians and educators to exchange experiences and ideas.

The following workshop plan serves as a template for professional development for educators, including librarians.

Outcomes

- Identify characteristics of youth with ASDs.
- Identify core educational challenges for youth with ASDs.
- Apply strategies for getting to know youth with ASDs on a personal level.
- Apply strategies for accommodating youth with ASDs in educational settings.
- Apply strategies for supporting appropriate behaviors of youth with ASDs.
- Collaborate with the service team of youth with ASDs.

Preparation

- Conduct the workshop in a room that is set up to accommodate youth with ASD: few distractions, distinct areas for different activities, and seating that is appropriate for youth with ASDs.
- Have on hand supplies that are useful for youth with ASDs: visual schedules, social-story binder, token system, Picture Exchange Communication System or other augmentative and alternative communication system, visual props, weighted belt or vest, assistive technology samplings, sample software or digital resources, and accompanying computers.
- Prepare handouts.
- Set up a display of resources.
- Set up presentation equipment (e.g., computer and projector, whiteboard and writing tools).
- Set up small-group communication supplies (e.g., newsprint, writing tools).

Summary of Workshop

Participants will learn about autism spectrum disorders and the typical behaviors of children in a learning environment.

> Presession activity
> 0:00   Introduction
> 0:05   Current knowledge
> 0:10   Background information about ASDs
> 0:25   Representative behaviors of youth with ASDs in a learning environment
> 0:45   Sample accommodations for youth with ASDs
> 1:15   Behavior management tips
> 1:45   Collaboration
> 1:55   Other resources
> 2:00   Closing

Presession Activity

Participants take an ASD quiz (see the Autism Spectrum Disorders Quiz at www.cdc.gov/ncbddd/autism/quiz.html).

Introduction

Welcome the participants and emphasize the need to work together to help youth with ASDs have successful learning experiences. Do a quick hands-up to see how many people know someone with ASDs. Then process the quiz and briefly discuss the answers. Emphasize that these are representative issues and that "to know one child with autism is to know one child with autism"—because there are so many reasons for ASDs and so many manifestations of them.

RATIONALE FOR CONTENT

Autism spectrum disorders are the fastest-growing set of developmental disorders in the United States, and about 1 percent of today's children are diagnosed with some form of ASD. Therefore, it is increasingly likely that librarians will serve this population. By better understanding ASDs and their manifestations, and how they affect youth relative to daily life, the more equipped librarians will be to work with them successfully. This workshop provides some basic tools to help make appropriate accommodations in mainstreamed educational settings.

ACTIVITIES CYCLE: EXPERIENCE, SHARE, PROCESS, GENERALIZE

1. Have participants share "Ten Myths about Autism" (www.abc news.go.com/Health/ColdandFluNews/story?id=6089162 &page=1#.TthUxfLeLzM and/or www.wrongplanet.net/article 361.html). Each myth can be posted on a separate card stock and shared in small groups.

2. Share one or more videos about ASDs from stakeholders' perspectives: For a doctor's perspective, see "What Is Autism?" (www.cdc.gov/NCBDDD/autism/videos/whatisautism.html). For a preservice education specialist's perspective, see "10 Things Every Child with Autism Wishes You Knew" (www.youtube .com/watch?v=AbeyIG7Fz8s); for a child's perspective, see "An Interview with an Autistic Child" (www.youtube.com/ watch?v=z8_Oi9UsgOI); for a parent's perspective, see "Autism: A Parent's Perspective" (www.youtube.com/watch?v=n7tCB 08bVvY). Ask participants to share their insights or new knowledge. Have the ASD expert answer possible questions or fill in knowledge gaps.

3. Share Sunfield School's PowerPoint presentation "Designing Learning Environments for Children with Autism," on ways to address educational needs of youth with ASD (http://eprints .worc.ac.uk/623/1/Seminar_Presentation_Tamara_Brooks .ppt). Group participants by age or academic discipline. Ask participants in small groups to write on newsprint how they might implement the strategies presented. Have the groups do a quick sharing of their ideas. Alternatively, groups can post their ideas, and all the participants can do a walk-around during a short break.

4. Share the Technical Assistance Center on Social Emotional Intervention for Young Children's PowerPoint presentation "The Pyramid Model for Supporting Social Emotional Competence in Infants and Young Children" (www.challenging behavior.org/do/pyramid_model.htm#presentations).

5. Watch the video "ABA Autism Classroom Case Study 2008" (www.youtube.com/watch?v=w9N0_7D_Re8). Stop the video after each case, and ask participants to state the challenge and the means to address the challenge. Alternatively, the video could be set up at several computers and paused before

individual cases. Each small group could discuss the case study in terms of challenge and solution.

APPLICATION

Explain service teams for youth with ASDs. If possible, have a service team member briefly state his or her role and function and how he or she collaborates. Alternatively, create a worksheet (see the box "ASD Service Teams") that lists team members and their functions for participants to match. Ask participants to identify their role in serving youth with ASDs and one other person with whom they might collaborate in support of that youth.

ASD SERVICE TEAMS

Directions: Match the service team member and his or her function.

1. Education specialist	A. Main advocate and first teacher
2. Special education aide	B. Academic content expert
3. Classroom teacher	C. Language diagnostician
4. School librarian	D. Expert on categorical funding
5. Reading specialist	E. Staff and crisis manager
6. Technology specialist	F. Cocurricular overseer
7. Academic or personal counselor	G. Tech manager
8. School psychologist	H. Most important person
9. School social worker	I. Social development expert
10. School health specialist	J. Researcher and resource expert
11. Activities personnel	K. Community resource coordinator
12. Site administrator	L. Personal helper
13. District personnel in charge of special education funding	M. Systems guider and supporter
14. Parent	N. Intervention planner and teacher
15. Child with ASD	O. Health counselor

Answers: 1-N, 2-L, 3-B, 4-J, 5-C, 6-G, 7-M, 8-I, 9-K, 10-O, 11-F, 12-E, 13-D, 14-A, 15-H

CLOSING AND NEXT STEPS

State that many human and material resources are available to help support youth with ASDs. If time allows, share some of the resources displayed or have each group examine a resource and do a brief "commercial" for the resource.

Ask each person to complete an evaluation sheet and state one action that he or she plans to do as a result of the workshop.

State any planned follow-up activity and implementation, and thank the participants.

RESOURCES

Note resources listed in the preparation and content section. This book's appendix has an extensive list of relevant websites.

ASSESSMENT

{WORKSHOP TITLE}

1. I thought the workshop activities were: *(circle the most appropriate term in each row)*

too basic	just right	too difficult
too slow	just right	too fast
uninteresting	interesting	vital!
irrelevant	possibly useful	just what I need

2. During this activity I learned:

a) _____

b) _____

c) _____

3. I will use this information to:_____

4. Now I want to learn: _____

5. During this activity I felt: _____

6. I just want to say:_____

VARIATIONS

1. If time allows, focus on the issues of room accommodations in Sunfield School's PowerPoint presentation "Designing Learning Environments for Children with Autism" (http://eprints .worc.ac.uk/623/1/Seminar_Presentation_Tamara_Brooks.ppt). Ask participants to think about their classroom or learning space as they look at the PowerPoint. After the presentation, ask participants to jot down one action they can do to improve their environment to accommodate youth with ASDs.

2. Have each small group watch a different video about ASDs and then compare notes. The differences can be by point of view, type of ASD, or different aspect of ASDs.

3. Have participants explore digital resources on autism.

4. Arrange the room so that participants sit at group tables. Have a service team member or a parent of a child with an ASD at each table.

TRAINING FOR LIBRARY STAFF

As with educators, library staff need to know the basics of ASDs and how to work with youth having ASDs and their service team. Most library staff have come into contact with someone with an ASD and may have some informal training, but they seldom are involved with individualized educational programs or frame ASDs in terms of library resources and services.

Depending on the size of the library staff, including volunteers, training can be somewhat casual. The underlying tone should be one of teamwork, where each person has experiences and skills that can contribute to the group's success in serving youth with ASDs and their service team. Therefore, the training can start out by having everyone share one fact or tip about ASDs and one thing that he or she would like to know.

After presenting some basic facts about ASDs, the group can then use a library perspective to brainstorm what contributions the library lends to the support of youth with ASDs and their service team: resources, referrals to community services, literature reviews, story hours, pro-gramming, meeting space, a safe social learning space.

At this point, library staff can brainstorm what resources they need to contribute significantly: more in-depth knowledge about ASDs, training in working with youth having ASDs, tips in behavior manage-ment, selection tools and bibliographies, relevant resources, assistive technology, supplies (e.g., visual schedules, AAC/PECS, social-story binders), modified furniture and space, additional funding, and addi-tional staffing or volunteers.

These identified needs can shape the kind of training appropriate to the group. Although it is tempting to have a onetime workshop on ASDs, it is usually more effective to offer a series of short, targeted trainings over time. In that way, participants have time to reflect and apply their learning, and to offer suggestions for future training sessions. It is also smart to enlist the help of local ASD experts in this process; developing and maintaining a positive, long-term professional relationship with someone in the field who works with youth with ASDs is a great way to facilitate community networking. Such experts can be found through school districts or public health agencies.

The project Libraries and Autism: We're Connected (www.libraries andautism.org) is the best-known library consortium addressing the needs of youth with ASDs. The project offers very useful resources and library workshop materials. Its two-part video on services to popula-tions with ASDs is particularly helpful (www.librariesandautism.org/video.htm).

TRAINING FOR PARENTS AND GUARDIANS OF YOUTH WITH ASDs

Parents of children with ASDs usually receive training from social ser-vice agencies, particularly with early diagnoses. Parents have in-depth knowledge and experience with their children and actively advocate for them. Nevertheless, they might not be aware of the role that the library can possibly play in their lives. Particularly since the library is a public space, even in school, some parents might be wary about exposing the public to their children if behaviors are challenging—or if the relatively strange space overwhelms the child.

As noted before, libraries can help youth with ASDs and their families become more comfortable with the facilities by giving individual orientations. Alternatively, librarians can videotape the tours and lend them to families to practice library manners. The most effective videotapes are probably ones that feature families that include children with ASDs interacting with other people.

Why would such families want to use the library? As mentioned already, libraries have resources about ASDs, stories written by and for youth with ASDs, community referral information, assistive technology, and digital materials. Libraries can provide programming such as story hours, teen clubs, speakers, workshops, volunteer opportunities, support groups, and community rooms. In addition, libraries serve as neutral public spaces in which youth with ASDs can be accepted and can have positive social experiences. Such information about library offerings might be best disseminated through flyers and online channels available in schools and public agencies.

In terms of training, a case may be made for offering workshops just for adults. However, target families usually do not have the luxury of attending events without their children. Instead, providing family events that include some informal training is the most feasible solution.

The most obvious type of training event is resource based: sharing reading. For example, a family story hour or reading event can share techniques for interactive reading. At the event, bibliographies of developmentally appropriate books can be distributed, and guidelines for choosing relevant reading materials can be provided. Likewise, an event about digital resources can engage families. A good technique is to incorporate the use of Smart boards to model engagement of youth with ASDs. As with books, a web-based bibliography of appropriate websites can be shared and posted on the library portal. Another event that would attract families is a "bring your own tablet" event to share ways to use iPads and other tablets and to suggest apps that work well for youth with ASDs. At these events, librarians can also display materials targeting parents to provide them with needed support in their daily lives.

These training events bring families and librarians together to develop positive relationships. They can also serve as a way for families to network socially with other families. Library-led community wikis could be established, inspired by a successful library event. Such synergy can lead to a library interest group that can assume the responsibility for future trainings and events about ASDs.

TRAINING FOR PEERS OF YOUTH WITH ASDs

As public spaces, libraries serve diverse and changing youth populations every day. Thus, a wide variety of youth may use the library alongside youth with ASDs. The more that young people learn about their peers, the more capably they can interact with them. In addition, youth-serving libraries are apt to use library aides, who can receive more in-depth training to serve as peer coaches for youth with ASDs. Librarians can work with classrooms, day-care centers, and youth clubs to provide information about interacting positively in library settings with youth with ASDs.

General Tips

Ideally, all youth should be explicitly taught about different kinds of people: age, culture, physical differences. Much of this training occurs informally as the occasion arises, such as seeing a person in a wheelchair for the first time. Librarians can offer tips to youth peers as situations arise in the library, such as the following:

- Don't be afraid of a person with an ASD.
- Treat him or her like everyone else.
- Sometimes a child acts differently, but he or she is still a child.
- Give them hints about social skills, such as raising hands.
- Say "Hi!" or start a simple conversation, such as talking about school or television.
- Ask a child with an ASD to do something with you or a group.
- Don't sneak up on him or her.
- Don't tease him or her; tell other people to stop teasing if you see that happen.

- Get the child's attention before telling him or her something.
- When trying to communicate, show rather than tell.
- Be patient with the child, and don't rush him or her; it takes time for him or her to process ideas.
- Compliment the child sincerely, such as saying "Great job!" or doing a high five.
- Offer to help, but don't do a task for him or her.
- If a child with an ASD acts funny, know that he or she probably can't help it and is probably stressed or anxious.
- Help remove the child from a noisy place if he or she becomes stressed, under the direction of an adult.

More formal training can also occur with designated groups, ranging from onetime basics about ASDs and expected behaviors to a research-based ten-part training for peers, such as Collis Adair's "Autism Spectrum Disorders" series (www.slideshare.net/chollisadair/autism-training -powerpoint-presentation). The trickiest part may be separating a mainstreamed group from youth with ASDs; however, youth with special needs are likely to participate occasionally in intensive intervention sessions, so that time can be used to train their peers.

Peer-Mediated Interventions

Because they are closer in age and development than adults, peers can sometimes provide interventions for youth with ASDs more effectively than adults can. Youth with ASDs can be close observers and are influenced by their peers' action; for that reason, mainstreaming youth with ASDs is usually preferred over special day classes. Youth with ASDs can identify with peers more easily than with adults because peers look more similar, talk more like they do, and act more like they do than adults. Peers are also less intimidating than adults.

Peer-mediated interventions usually involve interacting with peers to create and model social opportunities, teaching peer-specific social skills and autism initiation skills. Basically, peer-mediated interventions build on positive attitudes and supportive environments for social interaction. Peer-mediated interventions might consist of a peer buddy task, a designated playgroup, peer tutoring, or a group program (DiSalvo and Oswald 2002). Peers are taught basic information about ASDs and expected behaviors, specific intervention methods, how to initiate and facilitate social interaction, how to offer help, how to show affection and encouragement, and how to monitor and reinforce appropriate behavior (Chan et al. 2009).

As much as possible, peer-mediated intervention training should be voluntary. Fortunately, many youth are interested in service activities and want to make a difference in another person's life. Bellini (2006) noted several guidelines for selecting peer mediators:

- Choose peers with neutral or positive prior associations with the person whom they will help.
- Choose peers who respect and follow adult authority.
- Choose socially competent and responsive peers.
- Choose peers who act age-appropriately.
- Choose responsible and ethical peers.

Librarians should interview prospective youth and get recommendations, just as they would do for any responsible job. This process not only filters inappropriate individuals but also sends a signal that the function is important and valuable.

Circle of Friends

One well-established program (mentioned in chapter 7) is the circle of friends, which promotes inclusion and interaction with peers. This structure mobilizes youth to give support and problem solve with a person in difficulty, be it based on a disability or a challenging behavior. The adult helps gets the peer group started, meeting with them weekly for about a half hour to facilitate problem solving. A circle of friends typically becomes a self-sustaining group that needs little adult supervision after a while.

Even kindergartners can constitute a circle of friends. Here is a simple sequence of concepts to teach them:

1. Explain autism to the class. It is a lifelong disability that affects the way a person communicates with and relates to others.
2. Ask students to think of ways that they can help their classmate (e.g., involving him or her more and helping in class).

3. Illustrate ways to be clearer with their language.
4. Discuss ways to nicely correct their classmate if he or she does something inappropriate.
5. Allow students to give feedback about inclusion while reminding them about the link between their peers' behavior and ASDs.

Specific Types of Training

Training can also be customized according to the person's function in supporting youth with ASDs. In these cases, the first training can consist of an orientation to that role, and follow-up trainings can be crafted according to specific issues that arise (Seigel 2003).

Shadow aides are individuals who work one-on-one with youth with ASDs to help them adjust to a learning environment. Aides usually help individuals with specific academic and behavioral goals and monitor progress, under the direction of the service team. Shadow aides can be a great help to librarians because they can subtly guide and correct a child's behaviors in group situations so that the librarian can focus on large-group direction. Librarians should show shadow aides library procedures and expected behaviors in the library. They should also provide shadow aides with space to store the relevant supplies to address the needs of the child, such as fidget objects, token-system supplies, and augmentative and alternative communication resources. Ideally, librarians should work with aides and their supervisors to collect and maintain resources that can be used by several youth with ASDs and their service team members, including shadow aides.

Teen expert players serve as activity buddies for youth with ASDs. Their function resembles babysitting: keeping youth occupied and discouraging or redirecting repetitive, restrictive behavior. They can also introduce variety in simple sensory and motor activities. Teen experts are especially useful in the library during downtime or unstructured time, such as lunch and breaks; these times are often challenging for youth with ASDs, and the library is often more chaotic than usual at these times as well. Training teen expert players in the library usually consists of showing resources that might engage youth with ASDs, such as books that interest them and computer activities. To this end, librarians need to make sure that these teens know how to use the library catalog and locate materials, as well as how to log on and use the library's computers. Librarians should also instruct teen expert players on all of the library's procedures and rules and should show them needed supplies for youth with ASDs. They should also make sure that teen expert players have emergency and first-aid training.

Library aides help in many ways: processing and maintaining the collection, helping with displays and other promotional activities, helping with programming, providing technical expertise, and assisting users. Besides the regular library training, these aides need basic training in ASDs and ways to interact with their ASDs peers. The easiest way to approach this training is to have the library aides review each library task in light of the needs of youth with ASDs; for instance, what accommodations or special attention might someone with ASDs need when locating a book? Aides can role-play appropriate actions and brainstorm ways to make youth with ASDs more comfortable in the library.

It should be noted that teens with ASDs can serve as effective library aides. Particularly as transition plans are developed to help youth with ASDs handle postsecondary life, librarians can be involved in providing these teens with opportunities to learn valuable work skills. As with other library aides, teens with ASDs should be recommended for the job and be interviewed to ascertain whether the library is a good match as a workplace environment. These teens are likely to prefer having one stable task, such as shelving or book processing. The librarian should walk them through step-by-step procedures, preferably shown with visual reference sheets. Peer library aides can serve as effective coaches. At the beginning, these teens may need more supervision; a work checklist can serve as a reminder of duties and can help them self-regulate their work habits. They also need specific training on procedures for dealing with library users; providing them with scripted responses can help them feel more self-confident. However, once they have learned the library rules and procedures, and feel comfortable with their assigned task, these teens can be very reliable.

TRAINING RESOURCES

Increasingly, ASD organizations and state ASD-related agencies are developing trainings for stakeholders. Many of these trainings are free and online. The following list includes reviewed trainings, targeted to adults. It should be noted that not all trainings have been developed by professionals; well-meaning individuals such as parents of children with ASDs create trainings that might not be researched based. Although most training sessions are informative, their objectives have to be carefully considered to ensure that the training resource fits the audience and the task at hand.

Autism Classroom (www.autismclassroom.com) provides a series of downloadable training that complement the book *How to Set Up a Classroom for Students with Autism*, 2nd ed., by S. B. Linton.

Autism.esc2.net (http://autism.esc2.net/workshops.asp) provides scheduled free online workshops in English and Spanish.

Autism Internet Modules (www.autisminternetmodules.org) are expert-developed online free modules designed to promote understanding of, respect for, and equality of persons with ASDs.

Autism Society (www.autism-society.org/living-with-autism/how-we-can-help/online-courses.html) provides free online courses and tutorials.

DynaVox (www.dynavoxtech.com/implementation-toolkit/) offers videos, handouts, and other tools for providers to help youth with ASDs, particularly in product-based training.

Free Lecture Videos (www.freelecturevideos.com/tags/autism/#axzz1fPJWK7LV) has several online video presentations about autism.

Love to Know (http://autism.lovetoknow.com/Main_Page) provides slide shows on autism.

Positive Partnerships (www.autismtraining.com.au/public/index.cfm?action=showPublicContent&assetCategoryId=688) is an Australian organization that offers online resources for use in professional development programs.

Positively Autism (www.positivelyautism.com/aba/1about.html) has a free online tutorial about applied behavior analysis.

Techmatrix (www.techmatrix.org) is a searchable database for assistive technology, including professional development resources about autism.

Texas Statewide Leadership for Autism Training (www.txautism.net) provides several free multimedia online trainings about ASDs.

Virginia Autism Council (www.autismtrainingva.org) lists several free online training sites about ASDs.

REFERENCES

Bellini, S. *Building Social Relationships*. Shawnee Mission, KS: Autism Asperger Publishing, 2006.

Chan, J., R. Lang, M. Rispoli, M. O'Reilly, J. Sigafoos, and H. Cole. "Use of Peer-Mediated Interventions in the Treatment of Autism Spectrum Disorders: A Systematic Review." *Research in Autism Spectrum Disorders* 3 (2009): 876–89.

Commission on Teacher Credentialing. *New Special Education Added Authorizations*. Sacramento, CA: Commission on Teacher Credentialing, 2009.

DiSalvo, C., and D. Oswald. "Peer-Mediated Interventions to Increase the Social Interaction of Children with Autism: Consideration of Peer Expectancies." *Focus on Autism and Other Developmental Disabilities* 17 (2002): 198–207.

Seigel, B. *Helping Children with Autism Learn*. New York: Oxford University Press, 2003.

CHAPTER 10

Measuring Impact through Action Research

O DETERMINE WHAT INTERVENTIONS HAVE AN IMPACT ON LEARNING, both for youth with ASDs and for their peers, librarians need to be reflective practitioners, using action research to demonstrate their effectiveness. Once librarians determine their objective, they can conduct their action research: determining what to measure and why, identifying appropriate assessment tools, gathering and analyzing data, and acting on their findings.

WHAT IS ACTION RESEARCH?

Action research may be considered simply a systematic approach to identifying questions or problems in a setting and finding answers to solve or understand the issue. Action research differs from other kinds of research in that it focuses on one setting (or limited, related ones) and reaches conclusions that might not be generalizable as a result. Additionally, the action researcher is normally part of the picture as an insider participant. In terms of librarianship, action research may be defined as follows: "a systematic approach to investigation of a problem encountered in the daily library work environment, using methodologies that foster creating a detailed description of the context as reflected in the words and actions of the stakeholders and the library involved and that lead to effective solutions to the specific problem under study" (Cook and Farmer 2011, 12).

Action research typically follows these steps:

1. Focus on a topic or issue.
2. Review and synthesize the research and theory on the topic.
3. Develop research questions.
4. Collect data.
5. Analyze data.
6. Report results.
7. Design an action plan based on the data.
8. Take action.
9. Evaluate the action.

In the case of ASDs, librarians might want to provide more effective service to a specific person with an ASD or that population in general. Librarians might want to improve existing services to this population or investigate whether the library services positively affect youth with ASDs.

THINKING ABOUT METHODOLOGY

The research question drives the method to collect and analyze data. To investigate reading preferences, for instance, librarians would survey readers and perhaps their teachers, if in school. Although circulation statistics might be a convenient data-gathering tool, these measure only what people check out, not what they necessarily read. Nor do they indicate the reason someone borrows an item; it might be for a class assignment, for pleasure, or for a parent.

Traditionally, research methods tend to cluster into two groups: quantitative and qualitative. Quantitative methods usually measure the "what" of information about populations, with a tendency toward numerical data, such as test scores and collection statistics. The typical assumption is that the research builds on objective norms and abstractions of reality, which might apply to investigating youth with ASDs as a whole. Qualitative methods usually examine the "why" of information about populations through interviews and ethnographic studies of the population and their situation, and other phenomena-based approaches. The underlying concept is constructivist, and the context affects behavior and attitudes. Qualitative methods are most appropriate when trying to figure out solutions for an individual with an ASD. Current researchers tend to use both kinds of methods, a mixed-method approach, to get at the reality of an issue. It should be noted that several data collection tools can be used with a quantitative or a qualitative method in mind. For instance, surveys can measure both objective occurrences, such as how many books one reads a week, as well as perceptions, such as why one likes to read.

Once the action research objectives and indicators for evaluation are determined, the instruments for gathering evaluation data need to be identified. Here are some questions and appropriate data-gathering tools to answer those questions:

- How well do youth with ASDs write? Use content analysis of sample student work.
- How do youth with ASDs seek information? Observe their actions, and interview them.
- What interests youth with ASDs? Survey them.
- What do youth with ASDs think of the library? Survey them, and interview them (not in the library).
- How might the library better serve youth with ASDs? Conduct focus groups with their support teams, teachers of that population, and the youth themselves.
- How well do youth with ASDs read? Test them.

The choice of data collection tool also depends on availability, cost, and difficulty of administering and analysis. Ideally, the collection tool should be determined early on in the planning process, and assessment should occur throughout the effort.

Furthermore, the data are only as good as their analysis. Usually, someone on the support team has expertise in collecting and analyzing data about youth with ASDs. Librarians bring their expertise on information and research, as well as their personal knowledge of the child or population. Together, the adults supporting the individual or group can make sense of the data and use it to make informed decisions about treatment plans and specific interventions.

ACTION RESEARCH ON THE INDIVIDUAL LEVEL

To a certain degree, the members of the support team of each child with an ASD may be considered action researchers, because they collect and analyze data about the child, drawing on their expertise and formal study about ASDs and educational theory. Their diagnoses and treatment plans are monitored regularly and adjusted accordingly.

School librarians, in particular, should consider joining other support team members to find effective ways to help youth with ASDs develop their full self-potential. Librarians bring to the table their knowledge about literacies and research strategies. They can also locate appropriate assessment instruments and help collect data in their interaction with targeted youth.

Librarians can also spearhead such action research, especially to address a youth's literacy behaviors in the library. Here is a step-by-step example of one such action research effort:

1. Dana the librarian might observe a youth with an ASD, sixth grader Jeff, aimlessly surfing the Internet. Dana might want to help Jeff seek information more effectively.
2. Dana knows that the open Internet can be overwhelming for children; they may have difficulty creating a search strategy, identifying relevant keywords, determining the value and relevance of websites, and selecting the best resources. Dana also reviews the literature about information-seeking behaviors of youth with ASDs and finds out that these youngsters may have a limited vocabulary and a hard time comprehending what they read. Youth with autism can also have difficulties with loosely structured assignments.

3. Dana poses the research questions: How can assignments be structured to facilitate locating and selecting appropriate websites? How can the librarian structure the Internet experience to optimize information seeking?

4. Because Dana understands each step in information seeking, she can observe Jeff's information-seeking behavior at each data collection point. She can also examine the Internet browser history to identify Jeff's sequence of URLs, tags, keywords, and descriptions. Depending on Jeff's ability, Dana might also have Jeff do a think-aloud of his information-seeking processes.

5. Dana sees that Jeff has a limited vocabulary but good visual sense. She also notices that he has some trouble with the keyboard. Jeff is not able to evaluate websites well, and he judges their worth only by how colorful they are or some other detail that attracts him.

6. She looks for visually based Internet browsers and finds Zac Browser: an Internet browser designed for children with autism. Dana also finds out that the browser works with a Wii game remote control and checks with Jeff's support team to find out that Jeff has a Wii system at home to help him practice his balance. Dana downloads the browser and shows it to Dana's language arts and support team.

7. The teachers and Dana brainstorm a couple of ways that Zac Browser can support Jeff's learning, and Jeff's parents are willing to download Zac Browser at home to see if Jeff likes it.

8. Jeff enjoys Zac Browser, and the language arts teacher selects two websites from Zac Browser that Jeff can use in the class's next research project. Dana uploads the browser on the computer station that Jeff and the other students with ASDs use. Dana shows Jeff Zac Browser and makes sure that he can use it appropriately for the assignment.

9. The team, the language arts teacher, and Dana compare results. Jeff's effort on the research project shows more understanding of the desired concepts than his prior work. Jeff continued to look at the websites at home, using his Wii controller, which he preferred to the keyboard. Jeff also showed his preferred website to his mother. Dana also reported that she showed Zac Browser to a couple of other students with ASDs, with positive

results. Jeff still has trouble taking notes, so Dana says that she will work with the language arts teacher to see if another technology can be used for that task.

ACTION RESEARCH ON THE LIBRARY-PROGRAM LEVEL

Librarians can also investigate their library program of resources and services to see how they can be improved to positively affect youth with ASDs. What conditions for learning can libraries provide to improve student learning? Here is a starting list, based on extensive research (Farmer and Safer 2011), with implications for library programs supporting youth with ASDs noted in italic:

- Knowledgeable professional library staff with good interpersonal and communication skills: *librarians relate personally with youth and foster an inclusive library atmosphere.*
- Accessible library facility (school libraries have flexible scheduling): *operating hours are convenient for families and classes.*
- Current, relevant collection of resources: *materials meet the interests and needs of youth with ASDs.*
- Student access to Internet-connected computers and online subscriptions to databases: *databases are developmentally appropriate, and assistive technology is provided as needed.*
- Online library catalog and library web portal: *online library presence is developmentally appropriate and includes visual cues.*
- Librarian instruction competence: *instruction motivates and engages youth with ASDs, drawing on their strengths and interests and supporting academic progress; librarians effectively teach adults about library services for this population.*
- Regular and extensive collaborative planning and implementation: *librarians participate in support teams for youth with ASDs, and librarians collaborate with families and educators to provide resources, services, and instruction that support youth with ASDs.*
- Support for academic and recreational reading materials through materials selection, reading guidance, reading promotion, direct instruction, and support of other community read-

ing efforts: *reading promotion and support addresses the interests and wants of youth with ASDs.*

- Reference service: *librarians help youth with ASDs with their information needs, including teaching information literacy skills.*
- Community outreach: *librarians support families and partner with community agencies to support youth with ASDs.*
- Library policies, procedures, and a plan that includes assessment: *library policies and polities address the needs of youth with ASDs, and planning takes into consideration the needs of youth with ASDs.*
- Financial support: *funds are sufficient to build collections that support the interests and needs of youth with ASDs.*
- Administrative support: *librarians are given the funding and authority to carry out effective programs for youth with ASDs.*

Any one of these factors can be investigated to determine whether it is effectively serving youth with ASDs, with the intention of making the factors more impactful. The Lawrenceville (Georgia) Public Library's work in this regard exemplifies efforts to improve library programs to support youth with ASDs. Although its measurement of success predominately examines differences in library use, the librarians did include some anecdotes about impact on their clientele.

In the final analysis, librarians want to make a difference in people's lives. By conducting action research, they can collect evidence about current needs, develop a researched plan of action, measure the impact of their efforts, and share their work. In such a way, librarians prove their value in the lives of youth with ASDs, both on a one-by-one case and for the population as a whole.

REFERENCES

Cook, D., and L. Farmer. *Using Qualitative Methods in Action Research.* Chicago: American Library Association, 2011.

Farmer, L., and A. Safer. "Data Mining Technology across Academic Disciplines." *Intelligent Information Management* 3 (2011): 43–48.

The Perspective of a
Public Library

The previous chapters in this book have provided background information about youth with ASDs and issues that librarians need to consider when serving them. The book has also listed many resources and tools that librarians can use with these youth. This last chapter shares the success story of one public library that focused on the needs of youth with ASDs. Joyce Sands, Heather Sharpe, Karin Rezendes, Jen Richard, Beth Wagner, and Marti Pawlikowski are all librarians at Lancaster (Pennsylvania) Public Library. Their Autism Resource Center has provided effective services for youth with ASDs and their families. This is their success story, as written by them.

THE CORE MISSION OF PUBLIC LIBRARIES AND THEIR STAFF IS TO SATisfy the information needs of the communities they serve. This is the essence of our profession, and as public librarians we feel an enormous sense of frustration when we are unable to adequately respond to those needs. The staff at Lancaster Public Library felt that frustration when addressing the growing number of requests for information about autism.

In recent years, the number of individuals diagnosed as on the autism spectrum has dramatically increased. Experts in the field of autism continue to study the condition to determine its causes, to clarify the definition and characteristics of the disorders, and to refine the process involved in diagnosing this set of disorders, which affects all racial, ethnic, and socioeconomic groups. As a result, the demand for resources for individuals with autism, as well as their families, friends, and professionals who work with them, is also on the rise.

This increasing need became the impetus for creating the Autism Resource Center at Lancaster Public Library. The center is a dedicated space at Lancaster Public Library that offers a welcoming environment and houses a collection of more than eight hundred print, audio, and video resources as well as games and manipulatives. The center also has a laptop computer with Boardmaker software, a tool that visitors to the center can use to create the social stories, worksheets, and calendars used as adaptive aids to individuals with autism. It has a portable listening station that allows for four people to listen to either music or audiobooks. It also provides a video viewing station for previewing materials as well as entertainment for children while adults search for materials.

Opening the center was a costly undertaking. Like many other public libraries with limited financial resources, Lancaster Public Library's operating budget would not support the start-up costs associated with the center. The obvious solution was to apply for grant funds. In this instance, a Library Services and Technology Act (LSTA; Pub. L. No. 108-81) grant was the ideal fit. These federal funds are available through the Institute of Museum and Library Services, a federal grant-making agency, and administered in Pennsylvania by the Office of Commonwealth Libraries, the state agency for libraries. In 2009, Lancaster Public Library applied for an LSTA grant, and in 2010 it was awarded $32,000 for the project.

Preparing the grant application, and implementing the project once it was funded, required great teamwork. As soon as the decision was made to pursue the idea, an Autism LSTA Committee comprised of library staff was assembled. We began researching various aspects of the project, conducting focus groups, and connecting with community partners who provided valuable information on the subject of autism.

The process affirmed that there was a need for information that is easily accessible, current, relevant, and free. Families appreciated the idea of having a welcoming and safe space at the library that is devoted to individuals with autism, their families, and caregivers. Professionals, including therapeutic support staff, were interested in access to materials that could be used when working with their clients.

PARTNERSHIPS AND TRAINING

Research into what public libraries throughout the country were doing to serve the autistic community revealed that it was an area that public libraries had not yet embraced, despite an apparent need. Notable exceptions are the Scotch Plains and the Fanwood Memorial public libraries in New Jersey, whose directors, Meg Koyala and Dan Weiss, respectively, have been at the forefront of improving services to this underserved population by creating environments at their libraries that emphasize inclusion.

We first learned of their groundbreaking efforts when youth services staff members attended one of their workshops. Their website Libraries and Autism: We're Connected (www.librariesandautism.org) includes videos that walk libraries through the journey of service to users affected by autism. Through these resources, we became aware of the need for community education and staff awareness training. We partnered with Library Connections (www.libraryconnections.net), a consulting firm developed by Meg and Dan. They presented a customer service training workshop to the staff at Lancaster Public Library and surrounding libraries in and around Lancaster County. Through this training, the staff gained the knowledge necessary to recognize the behaviors associated with ASDs as well as strategies to effectively communicate with and serve individuals with autism. Staff learned that people with autism often struggle with communication. Routines are important to maintaining a purposeful outcome. One way to help individuals prepare for upcoming events is the use of social stories: a step-by-step visual of a procedure, visit, or task. These include simple sentences and supporting pictures (e.g., illustrations, icons, photographs) that examine a task from beginning to end.

Additionally, the youth services staff was provided training by another partner, the local Intermediate Unit No. 13 (a regional educational service agency), on Boardmaker software. An experienced teacher presented two separate workshops on how to use the software and provided practical examples of ways it can be used to assist individuals with ASDs.

It was very clear that an integral part of developing the center involved making community connections and developing partnerships. Not only were partners a necessity in the grant writing process, they also helped improve access to resources, ensuring that the needs of the community were met, and offered a cross-agency approach to addressing the needs and issues at large. It was through our partnerships with agencies such as the Intermediate Unit No. 13 and a local school district that we were able to tap into the expertise of several respected experts on autism. We also partnered with other autism agencies, therapeutic support staff, parents, and teachers.

COLLECTION DEVELOPMENT

We opened the center with approximately 550 print items, 100 DVDs, 20 CD-ROMs, 30 audio items, and 115 games. The collection also includes subscriptions to the periodicals *Autism Advocate*, *Autism Asperger's Digest*, and *Autism Spectrum Quarterly*. For the most part, locating print items for the collection was fairly straightforward. Several publishers specialize in autism and Asperger's syndrome, including Future Horizons (www.fhautism.com), AAPC (www.aapcpublishing .net), and Jessica Kingsley (www.jkp.com). These companies' catalogs are a good starting point for collection development, and most of their titles are available through large vendors (in our case, Ingram).

Our patrons' suggestions and needs were also factored into the collection development process. We purchased some materials that, though not directly related to autism, are of great value to those who use the center. For example, before the implementation of the center, our staff were frequently asked for materials on social skills and manners by the parents and caregivers of children with autism. Other related topics include discipline and gluten-free, casein-free cooking.

Additionally, we looked at materials used in the Intermediate Unit No. 13 and researched other library collections. Choosing which games and manipulatives to purchase was more of a challenge, but our community partners had many helpful suggestions and directed us to some great vendors, including Beyond Play (www.beyondplay.com), Different Roads to Learning (www.difflearn.com), and Got-Autism (www.got-autism.com). As with the print materials in the center, these items were purchased with the individuals with autism in mind, but they also can be used and enjoyed by any of the library's users (and any public library user countywide through interlibrary loan).

To differentiate the center's collection from the rest of the library's collection, we placed orange label locks over the spine labels of all items to be housed in the center. This labeling helped shelvers place the material in the right location.

Based on feedback from visitors to the center and survey responses, as well as the large number of audiovisual items in the collection, we purchased listening and viewing stations for use in the center. Users indicated that they wanted the opportunity to preview audio and video materials before borrowing them to ensure that the items met their expectations. Each station is equipped with headphones to allow for private listening and viewing. These also eliminate disruptions to other visitors of the center. This highlights the importance of seeking input from users and understanding the service from the users' perspective.

By reviewing current literature and interviewing parents and therapeutic support staff, we were also able to establish a need for tactile materials to serve this community. Comfort items such as weighted toys and other manipulatives designed to have a calming effect were suggested. Board games and other interactive materials were ordered to address social skills, memory, matching, and other basic developmental learning needs.

Families noted an interest in creating their own social stories around other community outings and visits to public places. To address this, the laptop computer was purchased and equipped with Boardmaker software. Having a copy of Boardmaker loaded onto the computer is especially helpful to those families not currently receiving services where they would otherwise have access. The program features thousands of symbols and can be changed to reflect forty-four different languages; therefore, those who speak English as a second language can use the program as well. The laptop can be borrowed and used in the library.

New materials are added to the collection on an ongoing basis, and materials in Spanish are added as they become available.

THE CENTER AS SPACE

The center is located in a room adjacent to the children's room that had previously been used as a study center. A large double-sided bookshelf was placed in the center of the room. One side contains all the print material, and the other contains the audiovisual material and games. There are also several tables that are often used by students and their support staff or parents to play games, read, or work on projects. The walls are decorated with art purchased from local artists with autism. A slat wall displays materials from outside agencies and organizations; brochures; featured books, magazines, and periodicals; and printed recommended reading lists for specific topics.

The center is open during all library hours and is used nearly every day. It is in a separate room located within easy view of and access to the youth help desk. The separate room eliminates distractions and creates a feeling of comfort and privacy for users of the center. Users can play games without fear of disrupting others. At times, visitors to the center have appreciated having a door to close while working with a loud or easily distracted individual. The enclosed space also allows an adult to browse the collection and feel comfortable knowing that his or her children are nearby and safe.

It's significant to note that, because of the nature of the disorder, it is equally important to ensure that the library is welcoming and easy to navigate. To make the entire library more accessible, signage was modified to clearly identify all collections, areas, and functions throughout the building. Many of the signs include both words and photos to accommodate those who benefit from visual cues. Our partners advised us on how the signs should be designed and the type of actions that should be depicted at each designated area of user service.

We recognize that making a personal connection with the users of the center is imperative. The location of the center makes it easy to see when it's being used, and if time permits, we make it a point to introduce ourselves, take time to listen to their situation, and begin a dialogue to guide them to the information they are seeking. It's also important to be available to answer questions and sometimes to act as a sounding board for users. We make a connection to typical behavior whenever possible (e.g., changes that are typical when entering adolescence may be thought of as part of the autism spectrum but are really changes most teens go through). We are careful to observe situations to prevent escalation into disruptive behavior by supporting the adults while redirecting or distracting the child. For example, a large visual timer is available to help a child anticipate upcoming changes, such as preparing for time to leave or ending a computer session. This appeases the child and gives the adult a few more minutes to look. As soon as the time is up, the adult and child gather their things and head out after a positive experience for all. We have learned to be flexible and make adjustments.

COMMUNITY OUTREACH

An important thing we recognize as public librarians is that we can have all the resources our community needs, but if the community doesn't know we have those resources, they might as well not even exist. Therefore, it is crucial to inform the public of what's available to them. Operating on a limited budget, it is difficult for public libraries to create pricey informational marketing pieces. Through the grant, we were fortunate to be able to fund the creation of posters, brochures, varied reading lists, and assorted promotional materials such as magnets and mouse pads.

Another consideration is that although it is ideal to have many resources, the size of the collection can be intimidating for users. With hundreds of books, how can they find the one that fits their needs? This is where public libraries shine. Public libraries have trained professional staff who can gather, consolidate, and organize information and resources. By creating reading lists, they can make it easier for people to find what they are looking for. Recognizing that there are many topics under the subject of autism, we created suggested reading lists for specific types of users (e.g., parents, teens, educators) and made them available in the center. We also published them on our website for easy access. We created a web page specifically for the center to include helpful links and resources, as well as a wiki with professionally reviewed and approved postings.

Getting the word to the agencies that the individuals with autism initially turn to for help is also of utmost importance. We need to understand where parents and individuals typically go for their information, and then make sure that these organizations know about the center and have materials they can distribute. Referrals are an invaluable way to inform the community; therefore, we maintain a database of interested community members who we can contact with news of the center. We designed a large portable banner describing the center for use in presentations at relevant events and in local schools and organizations.

Along with creating an environment throughout the library that is comfortable for individuals with autism, we created social-story books for preschoolers and teens. It was suggested that we create these stories to help guide users through a visit to the library. These are easily accessed and downloadable on our website so preschoolers and teens with autism can familiarize themselves with the library before visiting. Laminated, bound copies are available in the collection for circulation.

We have been active in sharing the information with other libraries as well, since this is not just a local need. Most of the resources are available for interlibrary loan so that many can benefit from the collection.

Another way to get the word out is to involve the media, and the key is to put the media on your side. Once the media sees how important the resource is to the community, they become more willing to provide coverage. An effective way for us to introduce the media and community to the center was through specific events and programs.

We held an autism awareness event as part of a national campaign, Light It Up Blue, to bring attention to the issue of autism. During this event we had various games and activities in our auditorium, and the center was open for browsing.

To build awareness and understanding in the community at large, we offered the program Autism 101. This program informed and educated the community on the characteristics and traits of autism spectrum disorders and possible interventions. We also invited author Nancy Patrick, who presented examples of two college students on the spectrum who gave video presentations on life with autism and the challenges and successes of navigating college life.

These programs brought people into the library, which then enabled them to learn about the many resources available through the center and generated media coverage that informed the public.

CHALLENGES

The library is a vibrant and active place, and it can be difficult to give users who have questions about the center the attention they deserve. And even with the suggested reading materials, users still have a difficult time finding exactly what they are looking for, because the call numbers are all very similar for a variety of subjects within the autism spectrum. We are considering reorganizing the collection and including signage that is more typical of a bookstore.

The logistics for using technology (e.g., the laptop with Boardmaker software, listening and viewing stations) has been challenging. We want to make the items available for use, but they are expensive, and we need to be concerned about theft. We also provide games, but it can be difficult to keep track of the many game cards and pieces. Finding time for staff to become proficient in the use of this and any future technology so that we can show users how to use it is also a challenge.

Although a large number of books is available for children with autism, their parents, and teachers, it is difficult to find books geared specifically toward teens and adults on the spectrum. Another challenge we face is the lack of Spanish-language material. We serve a large Spanish-speaking population, but we could locate only eight titles published in Spanish.

The grant excluded the purchase of fiction material, so the current collection comprises all nonfiction items. We would like to expand the collection to include fiction in the future, but this will probably require seeking alternate funding, such as another grant.

As with any large-scale grant project, sustainability is an issue. With the large amount of research being done in the field of autism, our collection will be out of date in a few years. Although our regular book budget allows for the purchase of some materials on autism, any large-scale update of the collection will have to be done using another funding source.

We also recognized the rise in the number of young children being diagnosed with autism, as well as an increase in the number of teens identified as being on the spectrum. As the population of diagnosed children ages, it is apparent that there will soon be a dramatic impact for businesses. As this population becomes consumers, businesses will need to attend to a variety of modalities, ranging from little or no eye contact to boundary issues. Additionally, this population will be entering the workforce, bringing along a new set of concerns for management. We felt it would be beneficial to hold a workshop for the business community to introduce them to the disorders they may likely encounter in the coming years and to provide some tools for them to apply to customer service and management techniques. We partnered with a business leadership network and arranged for an early breakfast program. This event was rescheduled once for lack of attendance. On a second attempt to present the program, we again had no enrollment and abandoned the effort. We concluded that we may have been a bit ahead of the business community in our awareness and that without having individual conversations with business leaders, it may take time before the reality of this projection takes place. And even then, it may require that an incident take place for the true understanding that they are not prepared to incorporate this demographic.

SUCCESSES

The best way to describe the some of the successes of the center is through a few anecdotes.

A young man with autism approached a staff member to ask about a book for teens about people with Asperger's dating. When a book on the subject was handed to him, he thanked the staff member with a big smile.

A mom was looking for a book about bathroom skills for her teenager, and she was relieved to see there was information available that could help her son.

One day a mother came into the center. Her son is on the autism spectrum and had recently lost services. She was overwhelmed and in need of direction. We pointed out a variety of materials to her. She was especially interested in social stories, so we also mentioned that we had Boardmaker, where she could custom make her own stories. We set her up at the computer, and she made a variety of materials to use with her son.

Another mother who attended all of the programs we offered was just becoming aware of the likely diagnosis of her young child. The overwhelming emotions that accompanied her realizations were calmed by the professionals she heard and the materials the library was able to provide to her.

Several parents have thanked us for our collection of games, DVDs, and software, noting that not only are the materials often too pricey to purchase, but none of the materials they desire come with a guarantee that a particular item will meet their child's needs. Providing them the opportunity to test-drive the materials prevents them from unnecessary spending.

We hear countless stories like these, and we realize that the center is not just a collection of books; the center is a resource that brings together many aspects of our community.

Another success is the significant increase in circulation of materials dealing with autism since the center opened. Before the opening, our collection had 168 items with a subject heading of "autism," "autistic," or "Asperger's." These items were checked out an average of 72 times a quarter. During the first quarter of 2011, items in the center were checked out 566 times, which is a 770 percent increase in checkouts of items dealing with autism. Of course, a big part of this increase is because of the large number of new items that were acquired, but it also definitively shows that there was a need for these resources in our community. Although our library was fortunate to secure grant funding for this project, an autism resource center or autism collection can be created on a much smaller scale. A small, core collection of materials can be of enormous help to a community.

CONCLUSION

We learned many valuable lessons when opening the center. Among those is the realization that although society in general and public libraries in particular have made great strides in accommodating the needs of individuals with physical challenges, we have not been as successful in meeting the needs of those with cognitive and developmental challenges. There is an enormous opportunity for public libraries to become leaders in the field of autism. Starting with organizational staff, educating people about the best approaches to interactions with people of any disability encourages acceptance and better understanding for the community at large. A welcoming environment promotes learning and communication.

In addition, we learned that individuals with autism and their families are in need of the materials necessary to gain a better understanding of the disorder and to discover strategies to overcome the associated challenges. These resources are expensive and can be difficult to find. This places a financial burden on families, and it costs them precious time. Having a collection of materials in one location that they can borrow free of charge can go a long way toward easing the strain on these individuals and their families. This is particularly true for those of limited means and without access to fee-based resources and services. Public libraries are uniquely qualified to provide this essential service to a growing population, and we feel a responsibility to provide access and lifelong learning to everyone in our community.

PROJECT TIMELINE

As mentioned previously, this project was a team effort that included the following:

- One adult services librarian
- Three members of the Youth Services Department
- One collection development librarian
- One public relations coordinator
- One deputy director

All members of the team had other responsibilities and worked on the Autism Resource Center project as time permitted. Because our project was funded by a grant, there was time involved in developing the grant proposal for submission to the funding body. The time allotted for the task was approximately two months. During that time, questionnaires were used to solicit input from the public, focus groups were conducted, and potential partners were contacted. Each team member focused on a different area of the project and wrote that portion of the grant proposal. One team member had responsibility for compiling the various components into a cohesive application.

From the time the grant was awarded until the center celebrated its grand opening, about six months passed. The timeline was roughly as follows:

First Month

- Convene a committee to meet every two weeks throughout the project.
- Contact partners to notify them that we would proceed with the project and to solicit their advice on materials and signage.
- Begin planning workshops with the partners who would be presenters.

Second Month

- Begin preparation of the physical space that the center would occupy.
- Identify items for the collection and begin ordering.

Third Month

- Receive items for the collection, and catalog and process.
- Purchase a laptop computer and Boardmaker software.
- Schedule and plan the grand opening.
- Schedule workshops for staff and the public.

Fourth Month
- Get bids for signage; evaluate and award the job.
- Begin to develop suggested reading lists.
- Develop marketing materials.
- Contact the media and send out press releases to begin to build interest.

Fifth Month
- Create surveys to be used once the center opens to solicit feedback.
- Develop surveys to be completed by workshop attendees.
- Conduct staff training workshop in advance of grand opening.
- Have signage installed.
- Send grand opening invitations.
- Arrange for speakers at grand opening, plan agenda, and finalize arrangements.

Sixth Month
- Host a grand opening event for the community, professionals, partners, autism groups, the press, elected officials, and library trustees.

Post-Grand Opening
- Host workshops for the general public, individuals with autism, their friends and families, and professionals.
- On the basis of user feedback, purchase listening and viewing stations.
- Launch a wiki for the exchange of information and ideas.

Autism Spectrum Disorders Education Resources

American Academy of Pediatrics (www2.aap.org/healthtopics/autism.cfm): The American Academy of Pediatrics' autism website discusses autism's characteristics and gives resources for parents, families, and professionals. It includes general resources and education materials.

Asperger Syndrome Education Network (www.aspennj.org): The Asperger Syndrome Education Network (ASPEN) provides families and individuals whose lives are affected by ASDs and nonverbal learning disabilities with education about the disorders' issues, support, and advocacy.

Association for Science in Autism Treatment (www.asatonline.org): The mission of the Association for Science in Autism Treatment is to share accurate, scientifically sound information about autism and treatments for autism. The association keeps a media watch and communicates through its newsletter and conference.

Autism Community (www.autism-community.com): The Autism Community strives to provide the most reliable and in-depth information on autism treatments and therapies to parents, teachers, therapists, and doctors.

Autism Genetic Resource Exchange (www.agre.org): The science arm of the Autism Science Foundation is the Autism Genetic Resource Exchange

(AGRE), this organization gathers and analyzes DNA and other medical data about autism.

Autism Information Center (www.cdc.gov/ncbddd/autism/index.html): The Autism Information Center is part of the National Center on Birth Defects and Developmental Disabilities within the Centers for Disease Control (CDC). The Autism Center provides information about ASDs and links to related projects within CDC and in other federal agencies.

Autism Institute (http://autisminstitute.com): The mission of the Autism Institute is to promote advances in the education of students with autism spectrum disorders and support national and state initiatives to build and sustain high-quality educational services.

Autism Link (www.autismlink.com): The mission of Autism Link is to provide opportunities for inclusion, information, and support; to keep autistic individuals, their parents, and their family members apprised of news and information, and to help them in their quest for services and in their quest for camaraderie with others in the autism community.

Autism National Committee (www.autcom.org): The Autism National Committee is an advocacy organization dedicated to social justice for all citizens with autism through a shared vision and a commitment to positive approaches. Their organization was founded in 1990 to protect and advance the human rights and civil rights of all persons with autism, other pervasive developmental disorders, and related differences of communication and behavior.

Autism NOW (www.autismnow.org): Autism NOW, the National Autism Resource and Information Center, is an interactive central point of quality resources and information for individuals with ASDs, their families, and other stakeholders.

Autism Research Institute (www.autism.com): The Autism Research Institute (ARI) conducts and fosters scientific research designed to improve the methods of diagnosing, treating, and preventing autism. The ARI also disseminates research findings to parents and others worldwide seeking help. The ARI data bank contains more than forty thousand detailed case histories of autistic children from more than sixty countries.

Autism Resources (www.autism-resources.com): Maintained by John Wobus, Autism Resources is a directory of information and links about autism and Asperger's syndrome.

Autism Safety Project (www.autismsafetyproject.org): The Autism Safety Project provides first responders, including families, with information and guidelines for communicating with individuals with ASDs in emergency situations.

Autism Science Foundation (www.autismsciencefoundation.org): The Autism Science Foundation is a nonprofit corporation intended to support autism research by providing funding and other assistance to scientists and organizations conducting, facilitating, publicizing, and disseminating autism research. The organization also provides information about autism to the general public and serves to increase awareness of autism spectrum disorders and the needs of individuals and families affected by autism.

Autism Society (www.autism-society.org): The Autism Society is a grassroots autism organization that aims to improve the lives of all affected by autism by increasing public awareness about the day-to-day issues faced by people on the spectrum; advocating for appropriate services for individuals across their lifespan; and providing the latest information regarding treatment, education, research, and advocacy.

Autism Speaks (www.autismspeaks.org): Autism Speaks is an autism science and advocacy organization, dedicated to funding research into the causes, prevention, treatments, and a cure for autism; increasing awareness of autism spectrum disorders; and advocating for the needs of individuals with autism and their families.

Autism Web (www.autismweb.com): Autism Web was developed by a community of parents interested in autism, pervasive developmental disorders, and Asperger's syndrome.

Autism-World (www.autism-world.com): Autism-World exists to introduce the knowledge of ASDs and to improve the community of autism. The website includes information about what autism is and how to diagnose and treat it. The website tells about newly developed research in this area, and helps parents of autism children cope with the disease.

Autistic Self Advocacy Network (www.autisticadvocacy.org): The Autistic Self Advocacy Network seeks to advance the principles of the disability rights movement with regard to autism. Drawing on the principles of the cross-disability community, the network seeks to organize the community of adults and youth with ASDs to have their voices heard in the national conversation about ASDs.

Collaborative Autism Resources and Education (www.educatorscare.com): Collaborative Autism Resources and Education offers English and Spanish services to support youth in social, emotional, and academic competencies. The website includes information about different programs and resources.

Council of Administrators of Special Education (www.casecec.org): The Council of Administrators of Special Education is an international professional educational organization that is affiliated with the Council for Exceptional Children, whose members are dedicated to the enhancement of the worth, dignity, potential, and uniqueness of each individual in society. The group's mission is to provide leadership and support to members by shaping policies and practices that affect the quality of education.

DisabilityInfo.gov (www.disability.gov): DisabilityInfo.gov, a collaborative effort of twenty-two federal agencies, provides an interactive, community-driven information network of disability-related programs, services, laws, and benefits.

Exploring Autism (www.exploringautism.org): Exploring Autism is dedicated to helping families who are living with the challenges of autism stay informed about the exciting breakthroughs involving the genetics of autism. It includes English, French, and Spanish-language resources.

Family Village/Autism (www.familyvillage.wisc.edu/lib_autm.htm): Family Village /Autism is a directory of autism resources that are geared to families and the community. It also includes non-English sources.

Fiesta Educativa (www.fiestaeducativa.org/home.html): Fiesta Educativa was founded in California in 1978 to inform and assist Latino families in obtaining services and in caring for their children with special needs. This partnership of families, professionals, consumers, friends, and agencies embraces as its mission the goal of universal support toward the enhancement of the lives of persons with disabilities. Its main program targets autism.

First Signs (www.firstsigns.org): First Signs is dedicated to educating parents and professionals about autism and related disorders.

Global Autism Collaboration (www.autism.org): Global Autism Collaboration is an organization created in response to a global need for networking and communication among autism groups. Although there are different perspectives among the autism groups, most share a common goal for a globally accepted standard of care and the elimination of discrimination. The goal of the collaboration is to disseminate information to organizations, which may, in turn, choose to distribute this to their members.

Interactive Autism Network (www.ianproject.org): The Interactive Autism Network is an online project bringing together tens of thousands of people affected by ASDs and hundreds of researchers in a search for answers. Individuals with ASDs and their families can share information in a secure setting to become part of an online autism research effort in the United States. The data collected by the network both facilitate scientific research and empower community leaders to advocate for improved services and resources.

Interagency Autism Coordinating Committee (http://iacc.hhs.gov): The Interagency Autism Coordinating Committee coordinates all efforts at the U.S. Department of Health and Human Services concerning autism spectrum disorders.

Interdisciplinary Council on Developmental and Learning Disorders (www .icdl.com): The Interdisciplinary Council on Developmental and Learning Disorders advances the identification, prevention, and treatment of developmental and learning disorders through its research, training, and publications. It provides the DIRFloortime Model.

International Rett Syndrome Foundation (www.rettsyndrome.org): The core mission of the International Rett Syndrome Foundation is to fund research for treatments and a cure for Rett syndrome while enhancing the overall quality of life for those living with Rett syndrome by providing information, programs, and services.

International Society for Autism Research (www.autism-insar.org): The International Society for Autism Research is a membership-based organization committed to sharing research on autism.

Libraries and Autism (www.librariesandautism.org): Libraries and Autism is the leading website for librarians who want to know about autism and how libraries can help.

LifeTips (http://autism.lifetips.com): LifeTips is a place to go for autism tips and hundreds of other related topics, such as social skills, sensory issues, treatment, public education, and funding.

National Association of Parents with Children in Special Education (www .napcse.org/exceptionalchildren/autism.php): The National Association of Parents with Children in Special Education provides a directory for resources targeted to parents. The autism page includes information on characteristics, assessments, interventions, and legal issues.

National Association of Special Education Teachers (www.naset.org): The National Association of Special Education Teachers is a national membership organization dedicated solely to meeting the needs of special education teachers and those preparing for the field of special education teaching. Among their publications is an ASD series, which includes overview information, assessments, interventions, and strategies for success.

National Autism Association (www.nationalautismassociation.org): The mission of the National Autism Association is to respond to the most urgent needs of the autism community, providing real help and hope so that all affected can reach their full potential.

National Autism Center (www.nationalautismcenter.org): The National Autism Center identifies effective programming and shares practical information with families about how to respond to the challenges they face. The center also conducts applied research and develops training and service models for practitioners. Finally, the center works to shape public policy concerning ASDs and their treatment through the development and dissemination of national standards of practice.

National Center for Technology Innovation (www.nationaltechcenter.org): The National Center for Technology Innovation assists researchers, developers, and entrepreneurs in creating innovative learning tools for all students, focusing on students with disabilities. Autism-specific technologies are included.

National Dissemination Center for Children with Disabilities (http://nichcy .org): The National Dissemination Center for Children with Disabilities is a database for research-based information to guide work with children with disabilities. About a hundred items address autism.

National Foundation for Autism Research (www.nfar.org): The National Foundation for Autism Research promotes the development of innovative treatment programs and options that improve the quality of life for children with autism and ASDs.

National Professional Development Center on Autism Spectrum Disorders (http://autismpdc.fpg.unc.edu): The National Professional Development Center on Autism Spectrum Disorders is a multiuniversity center to promote the use of evidence-based practice for children and adolescents with autism spectrum disorders.

Online Asperger Syndrome Information and Support Center (www
.aspergersyndrome.org): The Online Asperger Syndrome Information and
Support Center centralizes resource for families, individuals, and medical
professionals who deal with the challenges of Asperger's syndrome, autism,
and pervasive developmental disorders not otherwise specified (PDD–
NOS).

Organization for Autism Research (www.researchautism.org): The Organization
for Autism Research uses applied science to answer questions that parents,
families, individuals with autism, teachers, and caregivers confront daily.

Parents Helping Parents (www.php.com): Parents Helping Parents strives to
improve the quality of life for any child with special needs of any age, through
educating, supporting, and training their primary caregivers. Among other
services, it helps parents become effective advocates.

Pathfinders for Autism (www.pathfindersforautism.org): Pathfinders for Autism
is a parent sponsored, nonprofit organization dedicated to improving the
lives of individuals with autism and their families.

University of California, Los Angeles: The University of California, Los Angeles
(UCLA) has several centers that target autism. This university demonstrates
that higher educational institutions may address autism issues from several
perspectives:

- **UCLA Autism Intervention Research Network on Behavioral Health**
(www.asdweb.org)

- **Nathanson Family Resource Center** (http://nathanson.npih.ucla.edu)

- **Tarjan Center for Developmental Disabilities** (http://tarjan
center.ucla.edu)

- **UCLA Semel Institute for Neuroscience and Human Behavior, Center
for Autism Research and Treatment** (www.semel
.ucla.edu/autism)

U.S. Autism and Asperger Association (www.usautism.org): The U.S. Autism
and Asperger Association is a nonprofit organization for education,
support, and solutions. Its goal is to provide the opportunity for individuals
with ASDs to achieve their fullest potential.

Federal Government Centers

Several U.S. federal government organizations have centers that deal with autism.

Centers for Disease Control and Prevention: Autism Information Center
(www.cdc.gov/ncbddd/autism)

National Institute of Child Health and Human Development
(www.nichd.nih.gov/autism)

National Institute of Mental Health: Autism Spectrum Disorders
(www.nimh.nih.gov/publicat/autism.cfm)

National Institute of Neurological Disorders and Stroke: Autism
(www.ninds.nih.gov/disorders/autism/autism.htm)

National Institute on Deafness and Other Communication Disorders
(www.nidcd.nih.gov)

U.S. Department of Health and Human Services: Administration on Developmental Disabilities (www.acf.hhs.gov/programs/add)

U.S. Department of Health and Human Services: Interagency Autism Coordinating Committee (http://iacc.hhs.gov)

Regional Centers

Here is a representative list of regional centers that address autism. Particularly since legislation and regulations vary by states, service providers need to be able to consult local expertise.

Autism New Jersey (www.autismnj.org)

Autism Society of Connecticut (www.asconn.org)

Autism Society of Michigan (www.autism-mi.org)

Autism Society of Vermont (http://autism-info.org)

Florida Mental Health Institute (http://card-usf.fmhi.usf.edu)

Indiana Institute on Disability and Community (www.iidc.indiana.edu/index
.php?pageId=32)

New York ACTS (Adults and Children on the Autism Spectrum)
(www.opwdd.ny.gov/nyacts/nyacts_libraries_and_autism.jsp)

Virginia Commonwealth University Autism Center for Excellence
(www.vcuautismcenter.org)

Virginia Institute of Autism (www.viaschool.org)

California Autism Centers

This list of sample California autism service centers shows the variety of
services available and exemplifies the need to research local agencies, all
of which have unique resources. Most states have coordinating agencies.

Autism Society of America, Los Angeles (www.asalosangeles.org)

Autism Youth Sports League (www.autismyouthsportsleague.org)

California Department of Developmental Disorders (www.dds.ca.gov)

Cedars-Sinai Medical Center (www.cedars-sinai.edu)

**Children's Hospital of Orange County, Center for Autistic Children in Orange
County** (www.choc.org/ChildAutism)

Eastern Los Angeles Regional Center (www.elarc.org)

Families for Early Autism Treatment (www.feat.org)

Foothill Autism Alliance (www.foothillautism.org)

Frank D. Lanterman Regional Center (www.lanterman.org)

Harbor Regional Center (www.harborrc.org)

The Help Group (www.thehelpgroup.org)

Insurance Help for Autism (www.insurancehelpforautism.com)

Julia Ann Singer Center (www.vistadelmar.org/jasc.html)

Los Angeles Families for Effective Autism Treatment (www.lafeat.org)

North Los Angeles Regional Center (www.nlacrc.com)

Pasadena Child Development Associates (www.pasadenachilddevelopment.com)

San Gabriel/Pomona Regional Center (www.sgprc.org)

South Central Los Angeles Regional Center (www.sclarc.org)

Special Needs Advocate for Parents (www.snapinfo.org)

Spectrum Center for Educational and Behavioral Development
   (www.spectrumcenter.org)

Support and Treatment of Autism and Related Disorders (www.starautism.com)

Tri-Counties Regional Center (www.tri-counties.org)

Westside Regional Center (www.westsiderc.org)

Autism Blogs

Dozens of bloggers talk about ASD-related issues. Here are a few directories of such blogs. Most of these blogs reflect personal perspectives, so their experiences might not be generalizable. The most credible blogs are those sponsored by organizations, such as www.autisticadvocacy.org.

Autism Hub (http://autism-hub.com)

Autism Blog Directory (http://autismblogsdirectory.blogspot.com)

Autism List Autism Blogs (www.autismlist.com/index.php?c=13)

"A 05 Autism Spectrum Disorder." DSM-V Development: American Psychiatric Association. January 26, 2011. www.dsm5.org/proposedrevisions/pages/proposedrevision.aspx?rid=94.

American School Counselor Association. *ASCA National Model*. Alexandria, VA: American School Counselor Association, 2005.

Applin, M. "Instructional Services for Students with Disabilities." *Journal of Academic Librarianship* 25 (1999): 139–141.

Baker, J. *Social Skills Picture Books*. Arlington, TX: Future Horizons, 2002.

Bellini, S. *Building Social Relationships*. Shawnee Mission, KS: Autism Asperger Publishing, 2006.

Bennett, S. "First Questions for Designing Higher Education Learning Spaces." *Journal of Academic Leadership* 33 (2007): 14–26.

Bogin, J., L. Sullivan, S. Rogers, and A. Stabel. *Steps for Implementation: Discrete Trial Training*. Sacramento, CA: National Professional Development Center on Autism Spectrum Disorders, 2010.

California Legislative Blue Ribbon Commission on Autism. *An Opportunity to Achieve Real Change for Californians with Autism Spectrum Disorders*. Sacramento: California State Legislature 2007.

California State Department of Education. *New Special Education Added Authorizations*. Sacramento: California State Department of Education, 2009.

Center for Applied Special Technology. *Universal Design for Learning Guidelines Version 2.0.* Wakefield, MA: Center for Applied Special Technology, 2011.

Center for Universal Design. *The Principles of Universal Design.* Raleigh: North Carolina State University, 1997.

Centers for Disease Control and Prevention. *Autism Spectrum Disorders.* Washington, DC: Centers for Disease Control and Prevention, 2011. www.cdc.gov/ncbddd/autism/index.html.

Chan, J., R. Lang, M. Rispoli, M. O'Reilly, J. Sigafoos, and H. Cole. "Use of Peer-Mediated Interventions in the Treatment of Autism Spectrum Disorders: A Systematic Review." *Research in Autism Spectrum Disorders* 3 (2009): 876–89.

Cohen, Shirley. *Targeting Autism.* 3rd ed. Berkeley: University of California Press, 2007.

Commission on Teacher Credentialing. *New Special Education Added Authorizations.* Sacramento, CA: Commission on Teacher Credentialing, 2009.

Cook, D., and L. Farmer. *Using Qualitative Methods in Action Research.* Chicago: American Library Association, 2011.

Council for Exceptional Children. SpecialEdCareers.org. Arlington, VA: Council for Exceptional Children, 2011.

Courchesne, E., K. Pierce, C. Schumann, E. Redcay, J. Buckwalter, D. Kennedy, and J. Morgan. "Mapping Early Brain Development in Autism." *Neuron* 56 (2007): 399–413.

Courchesne, E., E. Redcay, and D. Kennedy. "The Autistic Brain: Birth through Adulthood." *Current Opinion in Neurology* 17 (2004): 489–96.

Dawson, G., D. Hill, A. Spencer, L. Galpert, and L. Watson. "Affective Exchanges between Young Autistic Children and Their Mothers. *Journal of Abnormal Child Psychology* 18 (1990): 335–45.

DiSalvo, C., and D. Oswald. "Peer-Mediated Interventions to Increase the Social Interaction of Children with Autism: Consideration of Peer Expectancies." *Focus on Autism and Other Developmental Disabilities* 17 (2002): 198–207.

D'Orazio, A. "Small Steps, Big Results." *Children and Libraries* 5 (2007): 21–23.

Farmer, L., and A. Safer. "Data Mining Technology across Academic Disciplines." *Intelligent Information Management* 3 (2011): 43–48.

Furth, H., and H. Wachs. *Thinking Goes to School: Piaget's Theory in Practice.* New York: Oxford University Press, 1975.

Gottman, J. *What Am I Feeling?* Alameda, CA: Parenting Press, 2004.

Grandin, T. *Thinking in Pictures.* New York: Vintage Press, 2006.

Gray, C., and J. Garand. 1993. "Social Stories: Improving Responses of Students with Autism with Accurate Social Information." *Focus on Autistic Behavior* 8 (1993): 1–10.

Greenspan, S., and S. Wieder. *Engaging Autism: Using the Floortime Approach to Help Children Relate, Communicate, and Think.* Cambridge, MA: Da Capo, 2009.

Gutstein, S. *Going to the Heart of Autism.* Houston, TX: Connections Center, 2004.

Hall, L. *Autism Spectrum Disorders.* Upper Saddle River, NJ: Merrill, 2009.

Harrower, J., and G. Dunlap. "Including Children with Autism in General Education Classrooms: A Review of Effective Strategies." *Behavior Modification* 25 (2001): 762–84.

Helt, M., I. Eigsti, P. Snyder, and D. Fein, D. "Contagious Yawning in Autistic and Typical Development." *Child Development* 81 (2010): 1620–31.

Henry, K. *How Do I Teach This Kid to Read?* Arlington, TX: Future Horizons, 2010.

Hernon, P., and P. Calvert, eds. *Improving the Quality of Library Services for Students with Disabilities.* Westport, CT: Libraries Unlimited, 2006.

Johnson, D., and R. Johnson. *Learning Together and Alone.* 4th ed. Needham Heights, MA: Allyn & Bacon, 1997.

Just, A., V. Cherkassky, T. Keller, and N. Minshew. "Cortical Activation and Synchronization during Sentence Comprehension in High-Functioning Autism: Evidence of Underconnectivity." *Brain* 127 (2004): 1811–21.

Kahn, J., E. Middaugh, and C. Evans. *The Civic Potential of Video Games.* Boston: MacArthur Foundation, 2008.

Koegel, R., and L. Koegel. *Pivotal Response Treatments for Autism.* Baltimore: Paul H. Brookes, 2006.

Leach, D. *Bringing ABA into Your Inclusive Classroom.* Baltimore: Paul H. Brookes, 2010.

Maurice, C., G. Green, and S. Luce, eds. *Behavioral Intervention for Young Children with Autism: A Manual for Parents and Professionals.* Austin, TX: Pro-Ed, 1996.

Minshew, N., J. Meyer, and G. Goldstein. "Abstract Reasoning in Autism: A Disassociation between Concept Formation and Concept Identification." *Neuropsychology* 16 (2002): 327–34.

Mirenda, P., and T. Iacono. *Autism Spectrum Disorders and AAC*. Baltimore: Paul H. Brookes, 2009.

Mostofsky, S., S. Powell, D. Simmonds, M. Goldberg, B. Caffo, and J. Pekar. "Decreased Connectivity and Cerebellar Activity in Autism during Motor Task Performance." *Brain* 132 (pt. 9, 2009): 2413–25.

Moyes, R. *Incorporating Social Goals in the Classroom*. London: Jessica Kingsley Publishers, 2001.

Myers, B. "Minds at Play." *American Libraries* 39 (2008): 54–57.

Myers S., and C. Johnson. "Management of Children with Autism Spectrum Disorders." *Pediatrics* 120 (2007): 1162–82.

Myles, B., M. Trautman, and R. Schelvan. *The Hidden Curriculum: Practical Solutions for Understanding Unstated Rules in Social Situations*. Shawnee Mission, KS: Autism Asperger Publishing, 2006.

National Association of Elementary School Principals. *Leading Learning Communities: Standards for What Principals Should Know and Be Able to Do*. Alexandria, VA: National Association of Elementary School Principals, 2001.

National Association of School Psychologists. *School Psychology: A Career That Makes a Difference*. Bethesda, MD: National Association of School Psychologists, 2003.

National Autism Center. *National Standards Project: Findings and Conclusions*. Randolph, MA: National Autism Center, 2009.

Notbohm, E., and V. Zysk. *1001 Great Ideas for Teaching and Raising Children with Autism or Asperger's*. 2nd ed. Arlington, TX: Future Horizons, 2010.

O'Brien, M., and J. Daggett. *Beyond the Autism Diagnosis*. Baltimore: Paul H. Brookes, 2006.

Odom, S., L. Collet-Klingenberg, S. Rogers, and D. Hatton. "Evidence-Based Practices in Interventions for Children and Youth with Autism Spectrum Disorders." *Preventing School Failure* 54 (2010): 275–82.

Odom, S., and S. McDonnell, eds. *Vanderbilt/Minnesota Social Interaction Project Play Time/Social Time*. Tucson, AZ: Communication Skill Builders, 1993.

Plimley, L., M. Bowen, and H. Morgan. *Autistic Spectrum Disorders in the Early Years*. London: Paul Chapman, 2007.

Porter, J. *Autism and Reading Comprehension: Ready-to-Use Lessons for Teachers*. Arlington, TX: Future Horizons, 2011.

Prizant, B. "Echolalia in Autism: Assessment and Intervention." *Seminars in Speech and Language* 4 (1983): 63–77.

Prizant, B., and P. Rydell. "An Analysis of the Functions of Delayed Echolalia in Autistic Children." *Journal of Speech and Hearing Research* 27 (1984): 183–92.

Prizant, B., and P. Rydell. "Assessment and Intervention Considerations for Unconventional Verbal Behavior." In *Communicative Approaches to the Management of Challenging Behavior*, edited by J. Reichle and D. Wacker, 263–97. Baltimore: Paul H. Brookes, 1993.

Prizant, B., A. Wetherby, E. Rubin, A. Laurent, and P. Rydell. *The SCERTS Model*. Baltimore: Paul H. Brookes, 2006.

Quill, K. *Teaching Children with Autism*. New York: Delmar, 1995.

Reference and User Services Association. *Guidelines for Behavioral Performance of Reference and Information Service Providers*. Chicago: American Library Association, 2004.

"Rett Syndrome." *PubMed Health*. Washington, DC: U.S. National Library of Medicine. www.ncbi.nlm.nih.gov/pubmedhealth/PMH0002503/.

Richman, L., and K. Wood. "Learning Disability Subtypes: Classification of High Functioning Hyperlexia." *Brain and Language* 82 (2002): 10–21.

Robinson, R. *Autism Solutions*. Don Mills, ON: Harlequin, 2011.

Rogers, S., and G. Dawson. *Early Start Denver Model for Young Children with Autism*. New York: Guilford Press, 2009.

Seigel, B. *Helping Children with Autism Learn*. New York: Oxford University Press, 2003.

Shriver, M., K. Allen, and J. Mathews. "Effective Assessment of the Shared and Unique Characteristics of Children with Autism." *School Psychology Review* 28 (1999): 538–58.

Sicile-Kira, C., and T. Grandin. *Autism Spectrum Disorders: The Complete Guide to Understanding Autism, Asperger's Syndrome, Pervasive Developmental Disorder, and Other ASDs*. New York: Perigee, 2004.

Simpson, R. *Autism Spectrum Disorders: Interventions and Treatments for Children and Youth*. Thousand Oaks, CA: Corwin Press, 2004.

Simpson, R., and B. Myles, eds. *Educating Children with Autism: Strategies for Effective Practice*. Austin, TX: Pro-Ed, 1998.

Sousa, D. *How the Brain Learns*. Thousand Oaks, CA: Corwin Press, 2011.

Spiegel, B. *Helping Children with Autism Learn*. New York: Oxford University Press, 2003.

Stokes, S. *Autism: Interventions and Strategies for Success*. Green Bay, WI: Cooperative Education Service Agency #7, 2001.

Tanaka, J., J. Wolf, C. Klaiman, K. Koenig, J. Cockburn, L. Herlihy, C. Brown, S. Stahl, M. Kaiser, and R. Schultz. "Using Computerized Games to Teach Face Recognition Skills to Children with Autism Spectrum Disorder: The Let's Face It! Program." *Journal of Child Psychology and Psychiatry* 51 (2010): 944–92.

Terrile, V. "Technology for Every Teen @ your library." *Young Adult Library Services* 7 (2009, Winter): 33–36.

Thompson, T. *Freedom from Meltdowns*. Baltimore: Paul H. Brookes, 2008.

Tomlinson, C. *The Differentiated Classroom*. Alexandria, VA: Association of Supervision and Curriculum Development, 1999.

U.S. Congress, Senate Committee on Health, Education, Labor, and Pensions. *Combating Autism Act of 2005: Report*. Washington, DC: U.S. Government Printing Office, 2006.

Vanderbroek, A. "RTI: The Librarian's Fairy Tale?" *Library Media Connection* (2010): 48–50.

Vasta, R., ed. *Annals of Child Development*, 8:1–41. London: Jessica Kingsley, 1991.

Wall, K. *Education and Care for Adolescents and Adults with Autism: A Guide for Professionals and Carers*. Thousand Oaks, CA: Sage, 2007.

Weaver, C. *Reading Process and Practice*. 3rd ed. Portsmouth, NH: Heinemann, 2002.

Wetherby, A., and B. Prizant, eds. *Communication and Language Issues in Autism and Pervasive Developmental Disabilities*. Baltimore, MA: Paul H. Brookes, 2000.

Wetherby, A., E. Rubin, A. Laurent, P. Rydell, and B. Prizant. *The SCERTS Model: A Comprehensive Educational Approach for Children with Autism Spectrum Disorders*. Baltimore: Paul H. Brookes, 2005.

Whitaker, P. *Challenging Behavior and Autism*. London: NAS, 2001.

Windman, V. "iPad Apps to Meet IEP Goals." *Tech & Learning* (2011, May 25). www.techlearning.com/article/39266.

Wisconsin Assistive Technology Initiative. *Assistive Technology Supports for Individuals with Autism Spectrum Disorder.* Milton: Wisconsin Assistive Technology Initiative, 2009. www.wati.org/content/supports/free/pdf/ASDManual-1.pdf.

Wolfberg, R. *Peer Play and the Autism Spectrum.* Shawnee Mission, KS: Autism Asperger Publishing, 2003.

Wong, P., and A. McGinley. "Rated E for Everyone." *School Library Journal* 56 (2010): 22–23.

Young Adult Library Services Association. *YALSA's Competencies for Librarians Serving Youth: Young Adults Deserve the Best.* Chicago: American Library Association, 2010.

Zarkowska, E., and J. Clements. *Problem Behaviour and People with Severe Learning Disabilities: The S.T.A.R. Approach.* 2nd ed. London: Nelson Thornes, 1994.

Americans with Disabilities Act (ADA): a U.S. federal civil rights law that prohibits discrimination based on disability.

aphasia: the loss of ability to comprehend or express language.

applied behavior analysis (ABA): a systematic behavior modification process that involves breaking down tasks into small achievable steps, each step building on the previous one, and using data to guide teaching and rewards, called reinforcers, for correct responses.

Asperger's syndrome: a disorder similar to autism, except that language is developmentally typical; one disorder among ASDs.

attention deficit/hyperactivity disorder (ADD/ADHD): a chronic condition that results in social, educational, or performance difficulties; symptoms include inattention, hyperactivity, and impulsive behavior.

augmentative and alternative communication (AAC): alternative methods used to help people with disabilities communicate.

autism: a developmental disability disorder that usually manifests with significant language delays, social and communication challenges, and atypical behaviors and interests.

autism spectrum disorders (ASDs): a spectrum of neuropsychiatric disorders characterized by significant social, communication, and behavior challenges

circle of friends: the use of peers to include and support a child or teen with difficulties.

Diagnostic and Statistical Manual of Mental Disorders (DSM): a publication including the official system of mental disorders used by U.S. mental health professionals for classifying psychological and psychiatric disorders.

discrete trial training (DTT): a part of applied behavior analysis in which complex skills are broken down into small, manageable steps; each trial has a sequence of three parts: direction, behavior, and consequence.

echolalia: repetition of the same word or phrase, sometimes echoing what another person says, to an extreme degree.

hyperlexia: the ability to read at an early age but usually without linking a word to its meaning.

individualized education program (IEP): a legally binding document written by parents and public education professionals that describes educational goals for student (over a one- to three-year term).

individualized family service plan (IFSP): a legally binding document that describes services for children younger than three years old with ASDs.

intervention: an influencing act that has the effect of modifying a person's behavior or attitude.

joint attention: the skill of looking at something of interest and sharing interest with another person; for example, a child looks at a person's eyes to see what he or she is looking at (social referencing) and follows that person's lead, or gets a person to look at what the child sees (e.g., points and says, "Look!").

mainstreaming: placement of a child with disabilities with typical peers in a regular classroom.

mand-model procedure: noticing the youth's focus of attention, providing a mand (yes-no question), and waiting for a response—then praising a correct response or modeling a correct response.

motor planning: the ability to plan and perform nonhabitual physical tasks, usually as a sequence of actions.

neurotypical: a term used to describe individuals who are not on the autism spectrum.

pervasive development disorder not otherwise specified (PDD-NOS): a type of autism spectrum disorder with some symptoms of autism or Asperger's syndrome symptoms but not enough for full diagnosis.

Picture Exchange Communication System (PECS): a program designed for early nonverbal symbolic communication training.

receptive language: ability to comprehend language.

Rett syndrome: a neurological disorder that affects girls almost exclusively; features normal development that then reverts, with symptoms associated with autism.

self-stimulation: behaviors done to stimulate one's own senses (e.g., rocking, spinning, hand flapping, echolalia).

sensorimotor: pertaining to brain activity other than the brain's automatic functions (e.g., breathing, sleep) or cognition; includes voluntary movement and senses such as hearing, sight, and touch.

shadow aide: an individual who works one-on-one to help youth with ASDs adjust to a learning environment.

social story: a short story that helps a child understand social situations and how to behave appropriately in those social situations.

spectrum disorder: a disorder that consists of linked subgroups of conditions rather than a single characteristic; symptoms can range from mild to extreme.